ADVANCE PRAISE FOR
THE HIGH ROAD

"Tommy Zurhellen is gifted, a truly gifted writer, a gifted humane human. And he understands how The Gift works, how it creates an economy that is in constant motion. His new book, *The High Road*, like his last book, *The Low Road*, recounts movingly and expertly the physical manifestation of this Gift and how, through Zurhellen's expeditions, it is propelled back into the world to circulate amongst us all, to bind us up, bound us each to each. *The High Road* is a chronicle of his performance of generosity, giving it all and not giving up. *The High Road* and Tommy Zurhellen are gifts that keep on giving. They work in our fractured and transactional world as a road map to kindness, an ocean chart through the sounded depths of hope."

Michael Martone
Author of *Plain Air: Sketches from Winesburg, Indiana*
and *The Complete Writings of Art Smith, The Bird Boy of Fort Wayne*

THE HIGH ROAD

Following the Campaign Trail for a Kinder America

Tommy Zurhellen

Epigraph Books
Rhinebeck, New York

The High Road: Following the Campaign Trail for a Kinder America © 2024 by Tommy Zurhellen

All rights reserved. No part of this book may be used or reproduced in any manner without the consent of the author except in critical articles or reviews. Contact the publisher for information.

ISBN 978-1-966293-00-2

Book design by Colin Rolfe

Epigraph Books
22 East Market Street, Suite 304
Rhinebeck, NY 12752
(845) 876-4861
epigraphpublishing.com

Midway upon the journey of life
I found myself deep within a mysterious forest,
For I had lost the well-traveled road.
Ah me! How hard a thing to describe
This savage wilderness lacking any kindness,
Which in the very thought renews the fear.

Dante's *Inferno*

AUTHOR'S NOTES

To write this story, I depended on my personal journal, social media posts, selfies and videos, news articles, follow-up conversations, research, and my own memory to recreate the events of my campaign for Dutchess County Executive in 2023. Some names have been changed, and some have remained the same. Some identifying descriptions of people, places or events have occasionally been omitted, composited, or altered to protect anonymity. You are encouraged to explore the "After/Words" section of this book, where I have invited many of the people who appear in this story to provide their own perspectives, in their own words.

This book is a sequel to *The Low Road: Walking the Walk for Veterans* which followed my solo trek across America in 2019 to raise awareness on veteran suicide and homelessness in our country. I highly recommend reading that book before diving into this one. All proceeds from both of these books go directly to help veterans in need, through Hudson River Housing's VetZero initiative.

This book is dedicated to the
13 million kids in America
who don't have enough to eat
and
the **everyday heroes** out there
trying to do something about it

Prologue
ABANDON ALL HOPE

NOVEMBER 7, 2023

It's Election Night across America and in Poughkeepsie, New York, I'm trying desperately to hide in a dark corner of a catering hall packed with hopeful candidates, local electeds, party officials, well-wishers and wannabes, as we all wait for the early returns to come in. A TV crew from News 12 idles patiently in the middle of the room, hoping for a few surprises as they wait for someone to win or lose. We're gathered at a place called the Pirate Canoe Club, which sounds like the perfect hideout for a scrappy bunch of Democrats trying to steal an upset victory from Republicans who have been in control of this county since, well, forever. At least we're located right on the banks of the Hudson River, so if things really go south, I can always head out into the autumn night air and just walk the plank. Nora and I are sitting at our table alone while everyone mills about, filling the room with loud chatter. She refreshes the screen on her phone now and again. Honestly, I'm too tired to stand. People have stopped coming over to wish me good luck. It's probably the surly look on my face, which right now hovers somewhere between *Go away, I haven't slept in nine months* and *Go away, I have uncontrollable diarrhea*.

Nora looks up from her phone. "Can I get you something to eat?"

"Let me guess," I say, closing my eyes for a moment. "Pigs in a blanket."

When she nods, I make a solemn oath to myself: after nine months of campaign fundraisers, potlucks, meet and greets, catered house parties, community picnics and backyard barbecues, there are now certain foods I will never under any circumstances put in my mouth again. Exhibit A: *pigs in the blanket*.

"They have the mushroom caps and little chicken toothpick thingies, too," Nora says, trying to be helpful. She doesn't know it, but she just introduced Exhibits B and C.

"I couldn't eat anything right now," I tell her.

"Okay," she says, smiling with a gentle shrug of her shoulders. Nora is probably just as tired as I am, but she doesn't show it. It's been quite a day for both of us. Together, we've crisscrossed Dutchess County, all 825 square miles of it, give or take. Our Election Day officially started at 6am in Rhinebeck with me dancing around the main intersection of town, tossing around a big sign that reads VOTE FOR A VETERAN! From there, we've hit a dozen other villages in the county doing the same thing. And our day ended only a few minutes ago, as I greeted commuters at the Poughkeepsie train station urging them to vote while getting interviewed on the platform by Spectrum News. We certainly worked right up until the final bell, when polls closed at 9pm. And to be honest, I almost didn't show up here tonight with all the other Democrat candidates; going straight home and finding out the results in the morning sounds a lot more enticing than sitting here to face the music.

If you've read *The Low Road*, then you already know Nora was a huge part of that adventure in 2019, as I walked across America to raise awareness on veteran homelessness and suicide. And it's safe to say she probably knows me better than anyone else here at the Pirate Canoe Club. She refreshes the screen on her phone once

November 7, 2023

again and suddenly her eyes light up, big as saucers. "Okay, here we go," she says, scrolling. "First results are in."

"I don't want to know," I say.

She scrolls some more and then stops. "Are you sure you don't want to know?"

"I don't want to know."

Before Nora can say anything, a party official on the other side of the room shouts out from behind his laptop. "All right, people, listen up! First results are coming in." He rattles off some early results on some local races. Then he gets into the four big county-wide races, including mine. "And wow, Tommy's up big!" The room erupts in cheers. People sound surprised more than anything. And I'm right there with them.

I look at Nora. "Is that right?"

She nods. "With 14% of the vote counted, you're up. By a *lot*."

In a flash, the TV crew darts over to our table and Baz, the reporter, asks me for an interview while his camera guy sets up the shot. After nine months of showing up at the same press conferences, Baz and I have become pretty good friends by now. But this will be the first time he's interviewing *me*. Baz says this will be a live feed, so we have some time for small talk before they switch to us from the studio, right after commercials.

"This is exciting," Baz says, looking around the room. "Frankly, we've never stayed very long with the Democrats on election night." He laughs and leans in closer. "Usually by this time, we're already setting up at Cosimo's to get all the Republican acceptance speeches." Cosimo's is a popular and posh two-story Italian eatery – excuse me, *trattoria* – located on the other side of town. It's the perfect backdrop for an election night celebration with high ceilings, Roman arches, and tasteful artwork on the walls. Yup, pretty much the exact opposite of the Pirate Canoe Club. Imagine prosciutto-and-fig flatbreads with a balsamic reduction instead of pigs in blankets; picture Negronis and prosecco poured with care by a mixologist named Fabrizio instead of Bud Light cans swimming in a big tub of ice. At Cosimo's, there's even a fancy staircase that provides the perfect photo op for acceptance speeches as a cheering crowd gathers below.

Baz perks up, tapping on his earpiece. "Okay, we're on in five," he whispers and before I know it, we're doing the interview. He does a quick lead-in before turning the mic to me. "I'm here with Tommy Zurhellen, Navy veteran and Democrat candidate for Dutchess County Executive. Tommy, early returns have you ahead in your race against your opponent, Republican Sue Serino. Are you surprised?"

Inside I'm saying, *does the Pope shit in a funny hat*? But after making it through nine grueling months on the campaign trail and doing dozens of interviews, I've earned the vital skill of giving polished responses in the slow, measured voice of a 3rd grade teacher. (Campaign tip: always look at the interviewer during an interview, not the camera.) "Not surprised at all, Baz. We've worked hard and I think you're seeing that work pay off tonight. As you know, we've been outspent 12 to 1 in this campaign, but that hasn't mattered. This year, the 'D' next to my name stands for Decency, and I think folks in Dutchess have responded to that. Listen, it's clear Dutchess County wants change after 32 years of the same people being in charge. But win or lose, we've already done so much to raise awareness on the issues people really care about, and I'm really proud of that."

Baz looks impressed. "So, what happens next?"

"Stay tuned," I say, trying on a smile. "But I really believe we are going to win."

Okay, that last statement is a big, fat lie because I showed up here utterly convinced we don't have a shot in Hell. Honestly, I don't know what to think. For weeks I've been telling myself if the election ends up being close – like, in the general neighborhood

November 7, 2023

of respectable -- then I should be satisfied. I just didn't imagine it would ever be *this* close. There is one thing I do know for sure: at this very moment, there's a bunch of well-dressed people over at Cosimo's watching the same returns, putting down their Negronis, and shitting a brick.

This is not going to be a story about politics. If you're hoping for one of those salacious political memoirs that promises to quench your thirst for naming names, settling scores, debunking conspiracy theories, unmasking villains, or taking you where the bodies are buried, you're going to be disappointed. This book doesn't have an axe to grind. This book will never wave its finger and shout, "You lie!" in the middle of the State of the Union address. This book doesn't pretend to know a whole lot about Watergate, Chappaquiddick or the Teapot Dome scandal. And this book doesn't want anything to do with dark money, dog whistles, photo-ops, super PACs, gerrymanders, pork barrels, perp walks, hatchet jobs, false flags, black bags, mudslinging, muckrakers or mugwumps. (Okay, I just had to google "mugwumps.") This book doesn't know anything about Robert's Rules. This book does not believe in dress codes. This book confesses it doesn't know the words to "This Land is Your Land," "We Shall Overcome" or even "God Bless America" and yet it has no problem belting out the entire theme song to *Scooby Doo!* three times in a row while waiting for the light to change. So, if you're looking for another blockbuster tell-all that simply reinforces your deep-rooted fears that the system is broken, our country is in the toilet, the other guy is always to blame, kids these days don't care about anything, homeless people are homeless because they want to be homeless, and Africanized killer bees are about to overtake America, I recommend you put this book down and just turn up the volume on the TV news instead. Anyway: you've been warned. This is not the book you're looking for. Move along.

Believe it or not, this is really a book about kindness. It's the underdog story of a middle-aged veteran who decided to plunge into the weird, mean-spirited mosh pit of local politics -- and the whole time, trying his best to be kind. If that sounds like a lost cause from the start, well, you're probably right. But aren't lost causes the only ones worth fighting for? Besides, this isn't my first rodeo when it comes to throwing myself blindly into a monumental mission for a good cause, with little chance for success.

It's my second rodeo, to be exact.

Back in 2019, I walked across the country alone to raise awareness on veteran suicide and veteran homelessness in America. That journey was the basis for my book *The Low Road: Walking the Walk for Veterans* and yes, the idea was as naive as it sounds. I bought a one-way airline ticket to Portland, Oregon and expected to walk back to my hometown of Poughkeepsie armed only with a mailbag, my VFW windbreaker, a phone, and some good intentions. That walk was born out of frustration: I had started to help veterans in my community, but I wanted to do more. A lot more. By day eight of the walk, I was ready to quit, and I wanted to go home. It was clear I had no idea what I was doing. But on that same day, I started meeting veterans on the road, usually far off the beaten path, and their incredible stories not only gave me the motivation to keep walking, they changed my life forever.

When the journey was all over, we had managed to share our story with more than 12 million people, thanks in large part to Nora's social media wizardry. That was years ago, but people still ask me questions about the walk. Where did you sleep? What did you eat? Did folks really send you 40 pounds of Nutter Butters at that tiny post office in Wyoming? (Absolutely!) But the question I get the most these days is a little more philosophical.

What surprised you the most by walking across America?

November 7, 2023

In a word: kindness. I was stunned at how many people treated a ragged, smelly stranger with genuine kindness, even before they learned the reasons for my walk. I grew up in New York City, so I was fully prepared to be run out of every small town in America with torches and pitchforks. *Get the ogre!* Or something like that. But I was completely wrong. In fact, the worst thing that happened to me after five months as a homeless veteran on the road was getting my walking stick stolen outside a Dunkin' Donuts in Ithaca, New York. Yup. That's it. And that's why my biggest takeaway from that adventure is the notion that people are inherently kind. That's not the story we get from political campaigns, for sure. We're constantly told we live in a fractured society, dog eat dog; but after all that time walking alone, I didn't see any of that. Instead, I only saw kindness. And it didn't matter whether I was walking through a tiny town like Kemmerer, Wyoming or a big city like Flint, Michigan. Everyone wanted to help. That's the real America I experienced. And that genuine show of kindness has stuck with me, even today. It's easy to see all the work I've done since the walk – for veterans, for people experiencing homelessness, for kids dealing with food insecurity – as my way of trying to pay that kindness forward.

When I was writing *The Low Road*, I used the classic tale the Odyssey as a framework to tell the story about the walk. It was an easy fit; after all, Odysseus and I were both veterans trying to find our way home. The book you hold in your hands right now is going to be a completely different journey, because *The High Road* isn't a story about finding home at all; turns out, it's the exact opposite. This book is going to be an escape attempt, an old-fashioned prison break. This will be a descent into a shady underworld most people have no idea exists, where the only reward waiting at the end of the journey is making it out with your soul still intact. It's a downhill slalom through the dark, mysterious subculture of American politics where the deeper you get, the weirder everything – and everyone – seems to become. I really mean that. And with a journey like that, it's obvious the Odyssey isn't going to cut it. No, there's only one classic tale which could serve as a proper frame for the crash course in politics I received in 2023. Of course, I'm talking about *The Inferno*, the wildly imaginative 14th century poem by Dante Alighieri that has basically given us all the things we believe about the underworld in western culture, from what the Devil looks like (bat wings, pointy tail, tricky disposition) to where sinners go within the Nine Circles of Hell (Ashley Madison subscribers? It's not so bad. Turncoats and double-crossers? I have very bad news for you.) It's the perfect scaffolding for our story, packed with plenty of gloom and doom. Now, I realize you might not have read Dante's *Inferno*, but I'll bet you know the famous inscription engraved on the gateway to Hell at the beginning of Dante's epic poem.

Abandon all Hope, ye who enter here.

Voices are getting louder as more election results come in. Some people are on their third or fourth beer and if it gets any more raucous in here, the Pirate Canoe Club could start living up to its name. It's still early, but there's already cause to celebrate for Democrats. Smaller races like mayor, town council and highway supervisor are beginning to be called one way or the other, eliciting thunderous war whoops whenever someone is declared an unofficial winner. There are some losers in the room, too – but knock on wood, Dutchess County Democrats seem to be on the verge of a very good night. Historic, even. So far tonight, we've elected the first Black mayor of Poughkeepsie – as in, *ever* – and we've also flipped a few coveted seats in the county legislature from red to blue. These early triumphs have this place buzzing as everyone crosses their fingers, mumbles prayers, and wishes for a blue wave

November 7, 2023

to finally wash over Dutchess this year. Across the crowded room, my good friend Yvette Valdés Smith just received a massive round of applause for utterly trouncing her MAGA-friendly opponent in her reelection bid to the county legislature. I don't know a candidate who has worked harder than Yvette these past nine months, so if anyone has earned an easy victory tonight, it's her.

I'm excited for her, but right now I'm too tired to show it. It's only ten o'clock but it's already past my bedtime. I want to sleep for a month. Baz and his TV crew pack up their gear after Yvette's big win, heading across town to Cosimo's to stake out the other sides' HQ in the Hudson Valley version of Capulets and Montagues. Baz comes over to say a hasty goodbye; with all the cheering, he has to shout in my ear. "Good luck! Who knows, maybe we'll be back," Baz says with a hopeful gleam in his eye. "I've covered elections in Dutchess for a long time, but I've never seen the Dems do this well."

It's going to be a while before they call the four countywide races, so I lean back into my chair next to Nora and close my eyes for a moment. With any luck, I'll fall asleep and wake up tomorrow morning. But when I open my eyes again, a paper plate has magically appeared on the table in front of me with some mushroom caps and chicken toothpick thingies on it, next to a cold can of seltzer. "You need to eat something," Nora says without looking up from her phone. "Could be a long night." She's laser focused on her screen, refreshing every few seconds for the latest updates.

"Okay," she says, titling her head to the side. "New numbers are in."

"I don't want to know," I say.

"Are you sure? There's good news and bad news."

I let out a long sigh. "All right. Give me the bad news first."

Nora pulls her chair closer. "Serino has pulled ahead, but it's still really close. Take a look," she says, showing me the screen. And sure enough, with 55% of votes now counted, somehow we are making this race for Dutchess County Executive too close to call.

How did this happen? How did a Democrat with no campaign experience, no money, and no connections find himself on election night running neck and neck for an office held by Republicans for the last 32 years? I want to know the answer to that question, and if you're still reading this book, I'm guessing you do, too. I don't have to tell you we live in an America where elections are usually won by fear. You win elections by scaring your voters to the polls, and also by scaring the other candidate's voters away from the polls. Why? Because fear sells. In America today, any candidate who wants to win tells voters how dangerous their opponent would be if elected, whether that information is true or not. He's going to raise your taxes! She's going to take your guns! They are going to put homeless people and addicts right next door! Then they connect their opponents to other people who they want you to be scared of: socialists, liberal professors, migrant workers, labor unions, Nancy Pelosi. Sound familiar? Stacy Abrams could give us a much better lesson in negativity bias, I'm sure, but I think we can all agree that as a nation, we've been conditioned to believe that kindness has no place in the savage world of modern American politics. You want to be kind? Go become a teacher, a nurse, a social worker, or a nun. Gumdrops and rainbows are great, but they don't mean much in political campaigns, where everyone seems to fight dirty. (That's what we're told, anyway.) So, it's no wonder millions of Americans feel disenfranchised when it comes to casting their vote. And with this grimy backdrop, it's crystal clear why nobody in their right mind would ever get into politics these days just to be kind. Ask any insider who works on a serious campaign today, and they will tell you that running solely on kindness would be a sort of political suicide.

Abandon all hope, indeed.

But what if someone did? What if someone challenged the

age-old notion that nice guys and gals always finish last? What would happen if there was a candidate who was determined to *only* focus on gumdrops and rainbows, a candidate who pledged to engage voters entirely with kindness and positivity, and never resort to the fear-mongering and negative attacks so pervasive in American politics today?

It would be nearly impossible. But hey, at least it wouldn't be boring. Right?

Well, that's what this book is really about. It's the story of nine months in 2023 when I tried to make it through a whole campaign without giving up or breaking down. And it's the reason I'm still sitting here with Nora at the Pirate Canoe Club on election night, waiting to see if all the work we've done will mean something.

The room erupts in celebration again with the news that my teammate Anthony Parisi has just been declared the winner in his race for District Attorney. Out of the four countywide candidates, Anthony had been given the best chance to win, but that's only because he and his wife (and amazing campaign manager!) Sinead worked their butts off. I know, because I witnessed that work every day on the campaign trail. Anthony's victory is especially sweet because he will become the first Democrat to become Dutchess County District Attorney in over 40 years. More evidence that Dems are having a huge night. It also means the results for my race can't be far away.

"New numbers are in," Nora says. "Do you want to know?"

"I don't want to know." I feel like I need some fresh air. I push myself up from the table and lumber towards the door, trying to sidestep the swell of people surrounding Anthony and Sinead as they celebrate an amazing win. As I reach the door, I can feel my throat tighten and my vision starts to get a little cloudy – both reminders that a good, old-fashioned panic attack could be on the way, once again. Yeah, a real doozy. I hear someone call my name, but I don't turn around. I walk out into the darkness of the cool

The High Road

November night. Half of me doesn't care if we win or lose; I just want this whole thing to be over. But the other half of me – the half that managed to walk across the country, the half made out of gumdrops and rainbows – wants to win more than anything in the world.

Can you win an election in America with kindness?

We're about to find out.

FIRST CIRCLE: LIMBO

EVER SINCE I was a little boy obsessed with comic books, I've assumed the public lives of our real American heroes – Captain America or Abraham Lincoln, Wonder Woman or Shirley Chisolm, fact or fiction -- all start with a bolt of lightning. Their stories seem to begin with an incredible twist of fate that usually takes place in an unforgettable setting. Maybe I'm just a sucker for a good origin story, but the way I see it, one day our champions are leading humdrum lives, and the next – *kazang!* – some Herculean challenge tests their mettle and pushes them towards a legendary lifetime of helping others. I'm thinking of Congressman John Lewis as a young man refusing to back down against violence and hatred on the bridge to Selma, sparking his career as a civil rights icon. And I'm picturing Ruth Bader Ginsburg as a young lawyer arguing her first case before an all-male Supreme Court, believing she would one day return to those hallowed halls and take her place behind the bench as an unequaled defender of women's rights. Throughout the history of America, our veterans seem especially prone to meeting that thunderclap of destiny; their incredible stories of sacrifice, courage and heroism so often become the very fabric of our nation, from future President Teddy Roosevelt leading the Roughriders up San Juan Hill, to young Navy Lt. John F. Kennedy saving his crew of PT-109 from capture in the South Pacific, to current U.S. Senator and decorated combat pilot Tammy Duckworth losing her legs to an RPG attack in Iraq and still insisting on continuing her military service for another ten years. (I don't know what your definition of toughness is, but Tammy Duckworth is mine.) Veteran or not, I've always imagined our social justice heroes get their start in a dramatic moment, ready-made for a future biopic or bingeworthy TV series.

That is, until now.

My origin story begins in an empty café tucked away between TJ Maxx and the Sew & Vac in a forgotten strip mall outside Poughkeepsie. It's the kind of place where capitalism goes to die. In my defense, I did not choose this location, and if I'd known this would turn out to be the meeting that sparks my journey into the wild world of American politics, I probably would have picked a nicer shirt. I might have even put on socks.

It's a few minutes before 8am on a chilly morning in early February. I got here early – I'm a veteran, I'm always going to show up early – and besides the nice lady behind the counter who took my order a few minutes ago, I've got the whole café to myself. I've never been inside this place before, and even though I've probably driven past on Route 9 a few hundred times, I never knew it existed until now. But the coffee smells like courage and I'm hungry for a real breakfast, which is rare. I went with today's special scribbled on a chalkboard: avocado toast and home fries. The décor is giving off a vintage speakeasy vibe, with weathered wood chairs, black metal light fixtures, and a big glass pastry case up front. The ordering system is old school, too; they give you a little numbered card when you order. When they call your number, you bring back the card to retrieve your food. Naturally, I'm number one.

My phone buzzes, letting me know the breaking news: a few minutes ago, Punxsutawney Phil saw his shadow, promising more dreary days ahead. After a while, the nice lady shouts out, "Number one!" in a voice so sharp it could guide an oil tanker through a dense fog. When I get to the counter, I'm trying to come up with a joke about calling my number even though we're the only people here, but the look on her face tells me she's in no mood for nonsense this early in the morning. So, I meekly take my tray back to my table and wait for the people I'm supposed to meet. A few more minutes go by, and my food is getting cold. These home fries need a friend. I'm still the only customer here, and I'm starting to hear the gurgles from my empty stomach.

A few days ago, my friend Amelia called me out of the blue to ask if I would have coffee with her and a friend, without telling me why. She told me the guy's name, but it didn't ring a bell. But I've taught the same classes at Marist for the past twenty years now, so any chance at intrigue is welcomed with open arms. Amelia and I are not especially close friends at this point, but I do know she's super-connected with the Democrats in Dutchess County and beyond. I'm almost certain she wants me to help another one of their candidates get more involved in the local veteran community, which is something I've done plenty of times for Democrats and Republicans alike the last few years. Why can't she take care of easy business like that over the phone? I have no idea. Some of these local politicians simply want a photo-op standing next to a veteran. Those are the worst. They will show up at the VFW with an entourage, take the picture, and then leave. To be fair, I've also connected with others running for office who have a sincere desire to do some real work and learn more about veterans in the community. It's refreshing to meet these public servants, because they are eager to do things like deliver meals to our veterans' shelter and even create new programs and workshops to help veterans across the county.

Amelia and I are still on the phone, trying to come up with a place to meet. "How about the Crafted Kup?" I say. This is a very popular coffee shop near Vassar College on the other side of town.

Fun random fact: it was also the location of my first date with the Fiancée! Our second date? Three hours of dancing at Spiegel Tent in the hot summertime. Yes, I lost thirty pounds of water weight that night, but I gained the reputation of a guy who will not give up. Our third date? Well, that's none of your business. And if you're reading this and you're wondering who the heck the Fiancée is, go back and finish reading *The Low Road* already. She is going to make a return in this book, so be ready!

"Not the Crafted Kup," Amelia says after a long pause. "Too crowded. Too many people around." Too many people around? If I wasn't already curious about this mysterious rendezvous, I am now.

"Where, then?" My local coffee shop knowledge is limited, I will admit.

"Let me think about it. I'll text you."

Later that day, she texts me with the name and location of the bistro I'm perched in now, which pretty much brings you up to speed on the reasons I'm sitting here alone, watching my breakfast get cold. I'm about to stuff a whole slice of avocado toast in my mouth when I see Amelia and a gentleman approach the glass door to the café. I say *gentleman* because at first glance, the guy trailing Amelia looks like he's straight out of a spy novel, one of those dashing characters you're not sure if they will turn out to be the hero or the villain, or maybe a little bit of both. When they both step inside from the cold I can see he's wearing a black turtleneck and herringbone jacket underneath his London Fog coat. His haircut probably costs more than my truck payment. His silver wristwatch probably costs more than my truck.

Amelia spots me in the corner and waves. They come over to the table, shaking off the cold from outside. As Amelia introduces us, I stand up and shake hands for the first time with the man who will come to be known as Big Papa. (For the record, he likes it when they call him Big Papa. At least, I think.) He takes off his coat and folds it with care over the back of his chair.

"Firm handshake," Big Papa says to Amelia, flexing his fingers. "Good sign."

With their matching blank stares, I suddenly get the impression I'm about to get the good cop/bad cop routine. I just can't tell which is going to be which. My stomach gurgles again, and I point back to the counter. "You guys want to order some breakfast?"

"No," Big Papa sighs, looking around the place. "We aren't big breakfast people."

I nod, getting up from my chair. "How about a coffee? I can get it for you."

"We don't drink coffee." He turns to Amelia again. "At least, I don't."

Amelia shakes her head. "No coffee for me, thanks."

I sit back down. Hmm. Maybe this is going down as bad cop/bad cop? Or worse, is this an intervention? Do I owe someone money? I can feel sweat beading on my forehead as I assess the situation so far in this ballad of the sad café: I was invited to a coffee shop by people who don't drink coffee. And I ordered this big-ass Hindenburg of a breakfast to sit with folks who, as it turns out, don't eat breakfast. Whatever is happening, I've suddenly lost my appetite. I slowly nudge my tray away. We might as well get to the point. "All right," I say, wiping my hands on a napkin. "Which candidate do you want me to connect with veterans this time?"

Amelia has a puzzled look on her face. She leans forward. "Tommy, we want to know if *you* would be interested in running for office this year."

I laugh, but only because I did not see this one coming. "You want me to run? For what?"

"County Executive," Big Papa says. "Top of the ticket this year. We have another possible candidate in mind, but Amelia thought you might be a good fit." He taps his fingers on the table and looks around the empty café. "So here we are."

"I thought Robin Lois was running for County Exec," I say. Robin is the current county Comptroller and one of the most popular Democrats around. She's actually one of those public servants I was just talking about who genuinely want to do the work to help veterans – together, we created a series of free financial workshops for veterans in Dutchess County that did a lot of good. And I had just assumed she would be the one to run for County Executive this year, because she's really the only person I can think of with a real shot at winning, especially in an "off-year" election.

"She's not going to do it," Amelia says. "We need to find someone else."

Ah. Now I'm getting the picture. They're looking for a warmish body to replace Robin Lois – and time is running out because the county convention, where they formally announce all their 2023 candidates, is only a few weeks away. Amelia must have pitched me to Big Papa as a possible Plan B – *Listen, this guy walked across the country! He's well known as a veterans' advocate! He's tall! He's a beloved professor at Marist! He can be funny – sometimes! And did I mention he's tall?* – and now Big Papa wants to meet me in person to see if I'm top-of-the-ticket material. And from the nonchalant attitude and frosty stare, it's obvious he's not very impressed so far. I can't really blame him; after all, he looks like an international man of mystery, and I look like the guy who is about to clean your gutters.

I look confused, because I am. "You said you had someone else in mind?"

"Yes," Big Papa says with another long sigh. "And no. They said they would only do it if we couldn't find someone else." He checks his watch again. "But here we are, finding someone else. So, we're not desperate. Yet."

"Who is it, if I may ask?" He tells me the name and I roll my eyes, because I do know the guy a little. "I thought you said you weren't desperate."

Big Papa lets out a cackling laugh like a Bond villain, startling me and Amelia both. "Oh, he's *funny*! You said he would be funny. I like him already." I've only known Big Papa for ten minutes, so I have no idea if this is his authentic laugh, or just his satiric, *go-fuck-yourself* kind of laugh. (Over the next nine months, I will come to know the difference.) A couple months later at my birthday celebration, he will tell me he walked into this coffee shop expecting to meet a guy with a boisterous, larger-than-life personality who could light up a room.

"And I did," he will say at my birthday. "It just depends on the room."

Our meeting at the sad café doesn't last much longer. I tell them I will think about it. "Think quickly," Amelia says. "The county convention is in three weeks." We agree to meet again in a few days at another covert meeting place, this time a local law office. Then Amelia and Big Papa slip out into the chilly morning air as quickly as they slipped in, leaving me alone again with two pieces of soggy toast and about a thousand questions churning in my head.

Am I ready for another huge challenge like this? Absolutely not. Let's do a quick inventory: I'm in the worst physical shape of my life. And my dance card is already chock-full of commitments, so many that I rarely have time to myself. I sit on three nonprofit boards and two veteran advisory committees. I deliver meals to the homeless shelter, I volunteer at the food pantry, and I help the Girl Scouts distribute cookies to veteran families through Operation Cookie Drop. And that's on top of the full-time professor gig at Marist for the past twenty years. I like what I do. I like doing things my way. And I love knowing I can make a real difference in my community. If I accept their offer, it probably means I won't be able to do any of that for the next nine months.

What do I know about running for office? Absolutely nothing. But to be fair, I had zero experience with walking across the country, too, and that seemed to work out okay. There's one vital difference between the two challenges, however; with the walk, I could have stopped at any time. I could have just decided to go home on any given day, just like Forrest Gump, and it would only have taken a week or two for everyone to forget the guy who *almost* walked across America. It's true I don't know much about political campaigns, but I do know this much: when you run for office, you automatically must consider the welfare of a lot more people than just yourself. Which means if I agree to start this journey, I will not be able to stop until I reach the finish line, win or lose. There's no crying in baseball, and there's no quitting in politics – at least, if you're doing it for the right reasons. If I say yes, there is no turning back. Too much is at stake. So, I'd better make damn sure I can find a way to see this thing through, no matter what.

I break out of my daydream long enough to realize I've been sitting here for so long, my butt is beginning to hurt. Outside the windows of the café, the sun has come up and across the empty parking lot I can see the commuter traffic building out on Route 9. I've got a few hours before I have to be at Marist, so I'm in no rush. I need to talk about this with someone. Who do I call? Perhaps the saddest element of this origin story is the realization that right now, I have no one to call. I haven't been with anyone since the Fiancée and for a long time, I've been missing that go-to person to share the big things, and the little things, in my life. That's not all bad; after all, there are certain advantages for a guy my age in living alone. But I also know there's a big difference between being lonely and being alone. When I think about it, maybe loneliness is one reason why I've overloaded my dance card with so many commitments to public service; because they fill an empty void inside of me, a pit I'm trying to fill with worthy causes where people want me. Where people need me.

First Circle: Limbo

Okay, that's enough self-pity for one day. This isn't going to be an easy decision, either way. Should I stay or should I go? There's the Angel standing on my right shoulder telling me, *sit this one out. Take care of yourself first.* And then there's the Devil on my left saying, *since when do you walk away from a challenge?* I can feel the pull from both directions. One thing's for sure: this is one road I would never be able to walk alone. It would be wonderful if I had a guide. It would be wonderful to have someone in my corner as I edge closer to that point of no return.

For a 700-year-old poem, Dante's *Inferno* is still a wild ride. Now, I don't know what kind of psychedelic drugs Italian poets had available back in the Middle Ages, but they had to be even more potent than whatever the Beatles were dropping when they wrote the White Album. The whole thing feels like a massive anxiety dream; the story begins with Dante himself being chased through a forest by lions, tigers and wolves (oh my.) The vicious beasts have him cornered in the dark wood but at the last minute, he's saved by the ghost of the ancient Roman poet Virgil, who was sent by Beatrice, goddess of love, who was sent by the Virgin Mary, who was sent by – well, you know. Virgil tells Dante there's only one way out of this nightmare: follow me all the way through the nine circles of Hell. Once you commit to entering the underworld, Virgil warns him, there's no going back. Them's the rules: sinners check in, but they don't check out.

And that's just the first chapter! What were you smoking, Dante? Whatever was in his pipe, it helped him create a magnificent fever dream and thrilling roller coaster ride full of chase scenes, double-crosses, suspense, twists and turns perfectly made for an 80s-era action movie with Arnold or Sly playing the hero. I can see the poster now: *Expendables 5: Highway to*

Hell. Personally, I see Jack Black as a groovy Virgil and maybe that guy from Poison as El Diablo himself when it gets greenlit for the obligatory Broadway musical. Anyway, Dante accepts Virgil's offer – how can he refuse when the alternative is being eaten by wolves? – and together, they begin their descent through the nine circles of Hell.

The first circle is called Limbo and as it turns out, isn't really part of the underworld at all. In Latin, the word "limbo" means boundary, and it doesn't house sinners; instead, it's full of honorable folks who just never got the chance to know the Christian God, like Homer and Aristotle and babies who were never baptized. Dante depicts this land as a sunny meadow, which I guess isn't the worst place to end up for eternity. As long as they have pickleball. To me, Limbo sounds a lot like the waiting room for a doctor's office, but a really nice one, with primo snacks and an Etch-a-Sketch for the kids. Limbo is actually Virgil's home turf, and he tells Dante that residents of this pleasant time-share village have a shot at making it to Heaven: Adam and Eve, for example, along with some guy named Moses.

We still use the word limbo today, of course, to describe any situation that's up in the air. Anyone who has felt the anxiety of waiting on a decision from their doctor, a judge, a CEO, a cop, building contractor or bossy spouse knows exactly what it's like living in Dante's version of Limbo. It's not Hell, but it's in the neighborhood. And right now, I definitely feel like I can fill up my own zip code with all the anxiety brewing inside me as I weigh the pros and cons of accepting this new challenge, or not.

I meet Amelia and Big Papa again as promised, this time in a borrowed conference room in the back of a cramped law office in downtown Poughkeepsie. I haven't slept much over the last few days. I've been busy calling all the people I trust in this world and asking their advice. (Luckily, the list is kind of short.) My first call is to Nora, to see if she would be available to help with the digital media portion of the campaign. Since the end of the walk, she's created her own digital media company down in Long Island, so she might be busy with other clients. "This would be my first political campaign," she says.

"Me, too."

"Let me do some research," Nora says, and through the phone I can already hear the gears turning in her head. "This could be exciting. Honestly, I thought you were calling to tell me you're doing another walk ... hey, *he walked so he could run*. How does that sound?"

"My first campaign slogan," I say. "You're the best."

Next, I meet Robin Lois for lunch to pick her brain but also to make sure she in fact doesn't want to run for County Executive. (She doesn't.) I call my cousin Ted who's involved in local politics across the river; I offer him a job – any job – if we get this campaign off the ground. I've also burned through about seventeen legal pads, drafting a never-ending list of pros and cons. But as of last night, the path out of Limbo still seems fuzzy and out-of-focus. I need clarity, and I don't really have anyone in my life who would be willing to go over seventeen legal pads worth of pros and cons with me, so I decide to bite the bullet and call the Fiancée. We don't talk like we used to but we're still good friends, and she probably still knows me better than anybody. I call her from my truck and we end up having a lengthy conversation that includes a lot of things that have nothing to do with me spending the next nine months kissing hands and shaking babies.

"I know you, Tom. You can't fathom doing something half-assed. If you are into something, then you're in all the way. It's the way you're wired."

"I'll take that as a compliment."

"It's not." She takes a deep breath. "If you say yes to this, you're going to throw yourself into it so completely, caring for yourself will take a backseat." Then her voice cracks and I can hear her start to cry softly. She puts the phone down for a moment to go find some tissues. When she comes back, we sit in silence for a while.

"I wasn't trying to make you sad."

"I know." She lets out a long breath. "Did you do your list of pros and cons?"

I look over at the legal pads stacked on the passenger seat of my truck. "Uh, trust me, I did. Hey, check out Pro reason #137: if I win, I get my own vehicle, with driver."

She surprises me with a laugh. "Funny, that doesn't sound like you."

Now I'm laughing, too. "See? I'm a politician already."

Somebody changes the subject and it's a good ten minutes before the Fiancée brings us crashing back. "You know you're not going to be able to please everyone, right?"

"I know." There is a long silence between us. Suddenly it feels like we're talking about questions that run a lot deeper than running for office. Old wounds flexing themselves to make sure they are not forgotten. "I've got to give them an answer tomorrow."

Another long silence. "Just answer this one question for me, Tom. Why do you want to run for office?"

"Because I can't sing or dance."

She moans, and I can hear her fist thumping against her thigh. "Seriously, Tom. Give me a straight answer. Why do you want to go through something like this?"

I take more than a few moments because I'm woefully out of practice talking about myself, especially with her. Old wounds, indeed. "I like helping people. And I'm good at it. These days, it's the only thing keeping me going."

"Now that sounds like you."

First Circle: Limbo

By the time we hang up, the decision feels a lot clearer in my mind. and I'm thankful for that. But I am even more thankful because the conversation with the Fiancée reminds me of two things: one, she's always had a world-class laugh. And two, when you spend seven years of your life with someone, there are certain things you build together that can never be torn down.

This time around, Amelia and Big Papa are the first to arrive at our meeting, and they look a whole lot happier than that dreary morning at the café. Chatty, even. Maybe this meeting will turn out to be good cop/good cop, who knows. Either way, I brought my own coffee, just in case.

"I'm your man," I say after a deep breath. "Let's do this."

They seem to be more relieved than anything. Which makes sense, because now they can stop wasting their time searching for another warm body, with the county convention only a couple weeks away at the end of February.

"Running for office is the loneliest thing you will ever do," Amelia says and I nod, taking in the wisdom of her warning. Of course, she's talking to a guy who walked across the country alone as a homeless veteran, so there might be some exceptions to that rule. But I'm keeping an open mind. I've got a lot to learn, and a lot less time to learn it. We spend the next two hours going over the basics of creating a campaign – everything from creating fundraisers to keeping financial records and finding a campaign manager. "Have you thought about your platform?" Amelia asks. I rattle off some issues I'm passionate about, living in Poughkeepsie. She shakes her head. "Start with housing. Voters want to hear about affordable housing more than anything."

Then she asks if I have any experience fundraising. "We figure you'll need to raise around $250,000 to have a chance against Sue," Amelia says. "How do you feel about that?"

"Sounds like a lot of money. Is that how much you think Republicans will raise?"

"Honey," Big Papa says with a smile. "They probably have that much already."

My jaw drops. This is the first of many moments over the next nine months where I will be reminded just how much political campaigns depend on the soul-sucking work of raising money. Amelia scribbles something on her pad, then she says, "Raising campaign funds will be a concern."

"Rome wasn't built in a day," Big Papa says with good cheer in his voice. He rubs his chin. "We've got to get you a sit-down with Roger Devereaux. Do you know him?"

"We've met a few times," I say. Devereaux is a prominent businessperson and philanthropist here in the Hudson Valley. We've stood on the same dais a few times when it's time to cut the ribbon on a renovated building or break ground on a new one. "I'm not sure he knows who I am, though."

"Doesn't matter," Big Papa says. "He knows your opponent, and I don't think they are exactly friends, shall we say." We start talking about the county convention coming up, and what I should be doing over the next two weeks before I officially accept the nomination for County Executive. "First impressions are key," he says, putting down his reading glasses to give me a once-over with a discerning eye. "This will be the first time people are meeting you in person. We'll need to find you a good blazer or two," he says. "What's your jacket size?"

Here we go. "I don't really wear blazers, suits, ties, stuff like that."

"Nonsense," he says. "What do you wear when you're teaching at Marist?"

I look down at my rumpled short-sleeved shirt with a hole in the pocket tucked out over a pair of tired, stretchy chinos. "Um, this?"

"We'll have to fix that. Where do you shop for clothes?"

"Oh, that's easy," I say. "The Big and Fat."

First Circle: Limbo

Big Papa starts to laugh. "You're joking."

But I'm not joking. I think the actual name of the place is *Casual Male XL*, but most guys who shop there just call it the Big & Fat. Back when we were together, the Fiancée would actually spend more time shopping at the Big & Fat than me, trying to make me look vaguely respectable. "It's down there on Route 9, right between the Goodwill store and Margaritas," I say, watching a confused look grow across Big Papa's face. "That's a Mexican restaurant."

He closes his eyes and rubs the bridge of his nose. "I see." Suddenly I feel like a husky Eliza Doolittle standing before a disappointed Professor Henry Higgins.

Amelia smiles. "Rome wasn't built in a day."

Two weeks later, I'm standing in a sea of people outside a middle school auditorium, waiting for the Dutchess County Democratic Convention to begin. This is it, the point of no return. I bought a blazer off the rack at the Big & Fat just for tonight. It's a bright metallic blue with little sparkles in the fabric, though, so I am reflecting light from all over the room. I feel like Joseph in the Technicolor Dreamcoat. My buddy Vince sees me from across the room and comes over. Like me, he is a true disciple of the Big & Fat. He runs his hand over the shiny sleeve fabric. "Now *that* is a nice jacket."

"You like it?"

"Like it? I *own* it. I'm so glad I didn't wear mine tonight, we would have looked like twins." Across the room, I see Big Papa talking to some people behind the check-in tables. It's loud in here, so I wave my hand to get his attention. After a little trial and error, he finally looks my way.

"See?" I say, pulling on my shiny lapel. "Wearing a blazer."

I can see a tiny sliver of a smile on his face. He rolls his eyes. "Congratulations."

There are about three hundred people here from towns all over Dutchess County. Officially, these are the delegates who will cast votes and create the 2023 slate of candidates for the county Democratic party; unofficially, they are gathered here to get excited about these new candidates. No one has told me I will be part of the festivities, so I'm sitting in the back row of the auditorium as a keen observer. My cousin Ted comes over and sits down next to me. "Nice jacket."

"Thanks," I say. "I'm getting that a lot."

People are taking their seats in the auditorium, and Ted takes a few pics of the gathering crowd with his phone. "So, you got your speech ready?"

I freeze. "Speech?"

"Sure, your acceptance speech. For the nomination."

I didn't know about any speech. At the very most, I was assuming I'd stand up when they called my name, smile and give my best beauty queen wave, before sitting back down. I start to get nervous, sweating through this beautiful new jacket of mine.

Breathe, big guy. Breathe.

As it turns out, I shouldn't worry so much because I'm not the only one unprepared. The convention is a loose affair, long on energy but short on organization, which is perfectly fine by me. Up on the stage, Big Papa does a masterful job as emcee, keeping the nominations for local offices moving quickly. When they finally get to the four countywide candidates – Anthony Parisi for District Attorney, Kenya Gadsden for County Clerk, Jim Rogers for Family Court Judge, and at the top of the ticket, some guy in a sparkly jacket named Tommy Zurhellen for County Executive – the energy has dissipated somewhat, with a lot of folks on their phones and a few in the back rows even falling asleep.

"We'll start with the top of the ticket," Big Papa says. "Here to

First Circle: Limbo

nominate Tommy Zurhellen as our candidate for Dutchess County Executive is our beloved Comptroller, Robin Lois!" Robin is sitting down front, but she quickly stands up with a confused look on her face. Obviously, no one had told her she would in fact be introducing me tonight; she doesn't want to get up there in front of all these people and just wing it, and I don't blame her. Luckily a friend of mine, Frank, volunteers himself to say a few words off the cuff about the big guy in the blue blazer. Short and sweet. (Thanks, Frank.) With that, Big Papa calls me up on stage, to some lukewarm applause.

It's true I don't have a speech prepared for tonight. But what I do have are a very particular set of skills, acquired over a long career as a teacher for the past 22 years. And that means I'm good at waking people up, getting them excited about the subject material (Jane Austen! Let's GO, people!) and keeping them focused for a whole class period. It's what I do. So, after all those years in front of a classroom, "winging it" is exactly what I'm good at. True, I might not be good at raising $250,000 in campaign funds. But I do have the power to get people to listen.

I take the mic from Big Papa and in my biggest, boomiest, most confident teacher's voice I bellow, "My name if Tommy Zurhellen, and I'm your next Dutchess County Executive." The snoozers in the back row start to wake up. I start to pace the stage like a self-help guru. People are putting down their phones, surprised more than anything. I pace back and forth some more, holding the mike to my mouth like I'm about to say something, then lowering it. (Laugh if you want, but if you want to build anticipation in a crowd -- especially college students – act like you're holding back a secret from them. Next time you're in church, you'll notice your favorite pastor is doing the same thing.) After a few more paces, I stop and turn to the crowd. "I only have one question for you tonight," I say, pointing my finger at random people in the audience. "Who's ready to get into some good trouble with me this summer?"

There's some polite applause, a few whoops and some people shouting back, "Me!"

I shake my head. "I said, who's ready to get into some GOOD TROUBLE with me this summer?"

Now I've got their attention. Most of the room is cheering and shouting back at the stage. One more.

"I said, who is ready for some GOOD TROUBLE this summer? Who's with me?"

Big Papa looks over from the corner of the stage, *who is this guy?*

Time for the big finish. "My name is Tommy Zurhellen, and I AM your next Dutchess County Executive. Good night." As I descend from the stage and walk back to my seat in the back, I get a standing ovation. I'm slapping hands and bumping fists with folks as I march up the aisle. As I sit back down, I say a hasty prayer to my hero John Lewis for giving us that powerful phrase *good trouble, necessary trouble.*

"Good speech," Ted whispers. "A little light on details, though."

"I'd better come up with more things to say, huh?"

He hits his forehead. "A platform. Good idea."

I listen intently as the other three countywide candidates are nominated and give their acceptance speeches. Sure enough, they're up there talking about actual issues and speaking in informed, measured voices, while I was up there selling snake oil. I've definitely got a lot of work ahead to become a real candidate, not just another salesman. At the end of the night, I get a chance to meet the other countywides for the first time. Anthony, Jim and I are all first-timers at political campaigns, and Kenya is running for County Clerk for a second time, in a rematch. I also meet Yvette Valdés Smith, who is the Minority Leader for the County Legislature running for re-election.

"What a jacket," she says.

And we're off. For the record, I will only wear this blazer – or *any* blazer – one more time during the campaign. Win or lose, I'm going to walk this journey being comfortable in my own skin. Tonight, standing in the same room with my new teammates and talking with them about strategy for the next nine months feels good. I don't feel like I'm waiting around in Limbo anymore; for the first time in a long time, I don't feel like a pretender anymore. I feel like I belong. And although none of us know it at the time, over these next nine months we will become a family, taking this journey together.

SECOND CIRCLE

THE FIRST thing they tell you to do when you're running for office is to get your headshots. These are the professional pictures that will get plastered everywhere over the next nine months, from your website to palm cards to bulk mailers (if you can afford mailers) so they'd better be good. You should smile but you can't look too happy. You should look confident but not too self-assured. You should appear poised but also comfortable in your own skin. Basically, you're telling a lie with your face. And the last time I posed in earnest for a headshot was my high school yearbook – white tuxedo, maroon bowtie – so this should be a great way to get used to the steep learning curve waiting ahead. I only really know one photographer in the Hudson Valley, so I give him a call. Tony has done a photo booth at our VFW charity events for a while now, and I break the news to him about my campaign for Dutchess County Executive, which is now officially two days old.

"Wow," he says. "What does a County Executive do?"

"I have no idea," I say, which is the truth at this point. But it's only the first week of March. "If I win the election, though, they tell me I get my own car and driver. So that's something."

"Happy to help, brother. What kind of headshots are you going for?"

I don't say anything at first because honestly, I had no idea there were varieties of headshots until this moment. "Can you make me look like a fun George Clooney?"

"Probably not," he says. "Rosemary Clooney, maybe." Tony is starting to understand I know zero about campaign headshots, so he gives me a quick tutorial. "I mean, there's all kinds of different things you can do. Indoor, outdoor. Sitting in an easy chair, standing in a factory with a hard hat, walking through a meadow. If you're big on the environment, you stand next to a river. Or if you want people to think you're a law-and-order guy, you stand in front of a shelf of law books. That sort of thing."

I think for a moment. "I do care about the environment. But it's twenty degrees outside, so maybe the meadow is out."

"Got it," Tony says. "Indoor it is." He tells me he knows another photographer across the river who will let him use her studio while she's away on assignment in Brazil. He texts me the address and we agree to meet there in a couple days. "Get a fresh haircut and bring a few outfit changes with you."

"I don't do suit and tie. Nothing formal," I say. "I don't want to look like something I'm not. I just want to look like a regular guy."

"A man of the people," he says. "I like it."

I visit my longtime barber (shout-out to my Navy shipmate Lee!) and pick out a couple of everyday shirts along with my black VFW jacket. I follow my GPS and to my surprise, it leads me to the parking lot of a daycare center; through the big bay window I can see they're in the middle of storybook time. Something about a frog. After a few minutes, one of the daycare staff comes out to confront the confused-looking guy pacing outside. Turns out, I don't have to say a word. "The photo studio is upstairs," she says before I can ask the question. She rolls her eyes with tired disdain and points around the side of the building to a wooden stairway. "Have a nice day," she snaps, already walking back. I'm wondering why the daycare lady is having such a rude reaction to the photo studio upstairs.

That is, until I see the studio. I climb the stairs and Tony ushers me into a large room with high ceilings, but it only takes me a second to realize this is not a normal photography studio. "My friend Lori mostly does boudoir photography up here," he says. "You know, getting into a character and doing a sexy photo shoot for your sweetie." In one corner, there's a long white fainting couch with a white bearskin rug draped over it, next to a table covered with veils and a 1930s telephone. The other has a blood red sofa surrounded by a forest of brass candlesticks. The back of the room is stacked high with all kinds of props. As in, sexy props. There are five different chandeliers hanging from the ceiling – I'm guessing one for each stage of grief. Even the powder room is made up to look like, well – a powder room. As I look around with my mouth agape, Tony is busy setting up his lighting umbrella. "We may have to move some of those candlesticks," he says.

I might have brought the wrong wardrobe choices for this shoot.

In the back of this book, I have included my official campaign headshot, which did indeed come from this same day. You will notice I am standing in a window, with some blurred, barren woods behind me. I am trying to smile. After Tony takes a few days to retouch this photo, I text it to Big Papa. He doesn't like it much, for a variety of reasons. (Number one, no blazer.) For the record, I kind of dig it. It looks like a guy you can lean on. It looks like me.

"And why are you standing in a window?" he asks me over the phone.

I make up some flimsy metaphor about opening a window of opportunity. I don't have the heart to tell Big Papa the real reason: that's the only spot in the studio where I wouldn't come off looking like Mata Hari.

"Nice smile," he says, trying to be diplomatic. "But you look uncomfortable."

Buddy, you have no idea.

"By the way, I have good news," he says, his voice perking up. "I talked you up to Roger Devereaux yesterday, and he wants to meet you." Good news, indeed! Wow. This campaign is going to be a lot easier than I thought: I'm only a few days into the campaign and I already have my headshots and now, a wealthy benefactor locked in. I mean, shucks, everyone has just been so darn helpful and nice so far! How far will this journey into the dark world of politics go until I finally get smacked in the face with a reality check?

Turns out, not long at all.

Before Dante and his guide Virgil can pass from the sweet meadows of Limbo into the Second Circle of Hell – the start of Hell proper, where the screams begin – they must get by Minos, otherwise known as the Judge of the Damned. Think the sorting hat from Harry Potter, but instead of sending young wizards to Hufflepuff or Ravenclaw, Minos coils his forked tail around each tortured soul to find out the sins they committed in life. Based on that infernal resumé, he transports them to the level of the underworld they deserve for their crimes. Hoarders? Misers? Fourth floor. Murderers? Moneylenders? Eighth floor. Traitors? Insurgents trying to overthrow a fair election? All the way down, boys. Mind the gap. Minos serves as the gatekeeper of Hell, forcing the wicked to confess their sins and spend the rest of eternity in *contrapasso* – that is, facing an ironic punishment that is the opposite of the sins they committed. Luckily, Dante avoids having to get wrapped in Minos' sorting tail; Virgil gets him off on a technicality because he's not actually dead.

To me, this whole scene in *The Inferno* sounds like an initiation – a gruesome one, sure, but an initiation, nonetheless. We've all been through initiations in our lives, from navigating the new job to meeting the spouse's family for the first time. As the outsider, isn't there's always a hazing element we put up with from the people already inside? Why we put up with it, I don't know. Maybe we just want to fit in, and we figure everyone else had to go through the same torture. I know I've been the FNG at countless points in my life – not just the Navy, of course, but everything from summer camp to becoming a professor at Marist. (If you don't know the term FNG, just ask any veteran, they'll get a kick out of it.) There always seems to be someone who fancies themselves a gatekeeper, that is, someone who believes it's their job to make sure newbies "earn" the right to be here. You know what I'm talking about. These are the folks who immediately shoot down new ideas because, well, they're new ideas. (These are also the folks who steal your lunch out of the fridge, but that's a separate issue.)

My own initiation into the weird world of local politics begins in early March, about a week after the county convention, when I get a message from my first social media troll. Pop the champagne! After all, you're not a serious candidate until strangers start sending you bizarre diatribes on Facebook. But this first troll isn't a stranger at all, and they're a Democrat, to boot. They write: *SADLY your campaign will NOT defeat your opponent. ALL of the Dems I speak to about your candidacy are SOOOOO disappointed.* Wow. I've only been the candidate for a week, so they must have started their research early. This same person will send periodic updates to this message throughout the campaign, to ensure I know just how disappointing I am.

The next day, a second troll tries to hit a bit deeper, this time via email. The rant is pages long so I will just share the highlights: *How did he walk across the country and not loose any weight? One day he's in Ithaca and suddenly he appears in Ellenville? Did anyone see him walk? I did the math, there's no way. And I herd *when he does the picnics for the Homeless he doesn't cook the food himself, other people do it. He always takes credit for stuff. You should invesigate him because he's a fraud.* The email is in third person because a copy was sent to a local reporter I know, who shared it with me just as a heads-up. Hey, it's my first conspiracy theory! I'm sad the email misses an opportunity to link me to the faked moon landing, the death of Princess Diana, and Bill Gates creating COVID in a Chinese laboratory. But on a serious note, I could have saved them some time by showing them every day of the walk was posted on Facebook, in real time, but they probably still wouldn't listen.

Anyway. Folks, the truth is out there.

My initiation continues when a week or so later, Ted calls to tell me a well-known Democratic party official named Terri wants my number to tell me something. I've met her a few times at events. "So, should I give her your number?"

"Did she say what it was about?"

"Nope," Ted says. "She wouldn't tell me. All she said was, it's really important."

I start to get nervous. Did I forget to file a form? Did I miss a meeting? Did the scandal finally break that I don't cook all the food for the homeless shelter myself?

Sure enough, Terri calls my cell an hour later. The suspense is killing me. "Tom," she says gravely. "I'm so glad I caught you. I'm sitting here with my sister. I've got something important I think you should know. Are you ready?" To me, it sounds like she's slurring her words a bit.

I steel myself for the worst. "Tell me."

There's a dramatic pause. I can hear some whispering in the background. Then she says, "Tom, I hate to be the one to tell you this. But you have dandruff."

Not what I was expecting. April Fool's Day is still a few weeks off. "Say that again?"

"You have dandruff. It's really bad. You have to do something about it."

"Okay. Is there something else you want to tell me?"

"No, that's it. The dandruff." Now there's laughter in the background. "Take care of that, okay?" And then she hangs up. It'd be one thing if this was just an anonymous prank caller, but this is an official in my own party who is supposed to be helping me win an election.

A few days later, Ted calls again as I'm leaving a meeting. He sounds exasperated, like he just stepped out of the ring after a few rounds with Mike Tyson. "You're not going to like this one, Cuz."

"Worse than the Dandruff Incident?" Yes, it's only been a few days but we've already immortalized Terri's weird call as the Dandruff Incident.

"It's way worse. You know Eunice in Rhinebeck?" I do know Eunice; she's in the same grassroots Democrat group as Terri. "She's hopping mad because you scheduled your fundraiser on the same day she wants to hold a meet-the-candidates event. She ripped me a new one. She wants to talk to you."

"Cuz, do *not* give her my phone number." A little background on this particular dumpster fire: recently, a good friend of mine graciously offered to hold a fundraiser for me at her beautiful home. Even better, she is good friends with a well-known singer/songwriter who lives in the area – if you're familiar with Tori Amos or Mary Chapin Carpenter, then you certainly know this person – and she's agreed to perform a short set at my event. Amazing, right? The only catch is, her touring schedule only allows one day in the fall that works, and that day is September 28, which is a good six months away. A lot of people are already looking forward to the event – including Big Papa, who is a serious fan of this musician, as it turns out.

A few minutes after I get off the phone with Ted, I'm still driving home from my meeting when the phone rings again. I don't recognize the number, but I can guess who it is. I mutter a few choice words before I pick up. "Hello, Eunice."

"Tommy. We need to talk." Her voice carries all the seriousness of a surgeon who just lost a patient. "You scheduled your fundraiser on the same day we are planning to have a meet-the-candidates event. You have to change the date."

I try to explain why September 28 is the only date we can possibly hold the fundraiser, but she's not having it. "We've already hired an artist to do the posters for the meet-and-greet, so we can't possibly move our event."

"It's six months away," I say. "Are you telling me you've already made the posters?"

"Well, no," she says, scrambling. "But we could have."

"Eunice, I can't move the event. That's the only day that works for the musician."

"Maybe I can talk to her instead and convince her to change the date. Do you have her number?"

"I don't." I honestly don't, but I wouldn't share it if I did.

But Eunice is dug in like a deer tick. "So, you're not going to change your event?"

"No, I'm not." Now I'm dug in, too. If she brings up my dandruff, all bets are off.

"Well, then," she says. There's a long pause. Then, Eunice drops the nuclear option. "In that case, we just might have to reconsider supporting your campaign."

That's right, she went there. Over a schedule conflict. Six months away.

"I guess you've got to do what you've got to do." Now I'm the one hanging up.

I call Big Papa afterwards and tell him what just happened, including the ultimatum at the very end. I'm more confused than angry. "Is this normal?"

"Sadly, yes." He gives me a quick history lesson about

Democrats in Dutchess County; some folks have been doing this a long time, and they are resistant to new whippersnappers coming in and rocking the boat. I get it. When I got to Marist twenty years ago as a young professor, the old-timers in my department treated me the same way. Sometimes they still do. Once I was told in a department meeting, "Anyone can teach creative writing." But that person was really saying, *know your place*. Just like Eunice and Terri, and the various internet trolls.

Big Papa's words go a long way to help me understand this confusing world I have entered, and I am thankful for his help. "I'll talk Eunice off the ledge," he says. "You won't have to move your event." He must sense my disappointment. "Don't waste time worrying about these things. They're going to happen, so get used to it. Focus on the important things, like your meeting with Devereaux and the candidates' forum in Pine Plains at the end of the month. You've got to ace both of those." He's right, of course. Don't sweat the small stuff. After we hang up, I have even more respect for the man because I realize 98% of his job must talking to cranky people and smoothing things over between people who are supposed to be working together.

In other words, herding cats.

I arrange to meet Roger Devereaux for lunch at a cafeteria across the street from my office at Marist. He's late, but for late March it's a beautiful day outside, and even though I have class in an hour, I don't mind waiting for the guy because I still have no idea what I'm going to say for my campaign pitch. I'm half-expecting him to pull up in a fancy limousine or enormous SUV complete with entourage, but instead it's just him, driving a very normal car. I should know better, since we've met a few times before; he carries an old school flip-phone and wears off-the-rack clothes, too, completing the Warren Buffet vibe. Meeting today at Marist for lunch was his idea. "I don't get a chance to see campus as much as I'd like," he told me over the phone. I don't know much about him, other than what Big Papa tells me, but I do know if you're a nonprofit in the Hudson Valley, you've probably asked his foundation for money. I know, because I serve on the Board of Directors at three of those nonprofits right now, and let's just say I've heard his name come up more than once.

We're standing in line inside the cafeteria, sharing the usual first-date small talk. He seems like a no-nonsense type of guy, which is right up my alley. The line up to the counter isn't long but there's a lot of students in here, picking up the food they ordered on their phones. Roger asks me about my classes, the walk, and my time in the Navy. I tell him a couple of quick Navy stories before we get to the counter and the young woman at the register asks for our order.

"I've got this," I say, reaching for my Marist Money card.

"No, I insist," he says quickly. "I'd like a hamburger," he says to the cashier, which unleashes a barrage of questions from the kid behind the register. Cheese? Grilled onions? Lettuce? Tomato? Roger gives her a confused look; I get the feeling this guy doesn't find himself ordering food over a cafeteria counter very often. "No, I'd just like a regular, All-American hamburger. Can you do that?"

"We can," the woman says cheerily. I order a chicken sandwich and a seltzer. She gives Roger the total and he pulls out his Amex from a weathered wallet. The card doesn't go through after the first try, or the second, or the third. I want to say I'm pretty sure they don't see a lot of *American Express Triple Uranium* cards at this cafeteria, but I don't because I can see Devereaux is starting to get visibly annoyed. The cashier turns and yells for the manager to come over.

As we wait, Roger leans over to me. "Maybe if I told them my name is on the building over there," he whispers. "We might get out of here faster."

The manager gives it a go with the card reader, but no luck. Finally, Roger pulls out another credit card and it goes through like a charm. We grab our trays and find a table tucked away in the back corner. He's already asked me a ton of questions, but I haven't learned anything about him yet, except for the fact he likes ketchup on his burger. A lot of it.

"So, have you thought about your platform?" he says as we eat.

Here we go! I put my sandwich down because I'm about to deliver a long, noble, well-rehearsed elevator pitch about running on kindness. "Well, Mr. Devereaux, I have such a passion for –"

"Call me Roger. Here's your platform, okay?" he says, holding out his palm and raising his fingers, one by one. "Housing, housing, and housing. Affordable housing is what people care most about. Only, don't call it that. Call it *workforce* housing. You call it affordable housing and they think you're going to build a homeless shelter next door. Nobody wants that, right? So, building workforce housing. That's the key. Got it?"

"Workforce housing," I say, nodding. "Got it."

"And stay away from all that bleeding heart, liberal, save the whales crap," he says, looking out the window at the students streaming by. "Taxpayers don't want to hear that."

"No whales," I say. "Got it."

He looks out the window for a spell. "Tommy, I'm going to help you. You're my guy. I'm going to help you raise $100,000 and you're going to win this thing." He looks at my rumpled shirt, now with chicken sandwich crumbs on it. "You own some suits?"

"I don't," I say. "I do have a blazer though."

"Well, get yourself some suits. Dark blue. No one's going to take you seriously, looking like this." I check my watch; I have to teach in a few minutes, so we finish our lunch and continue the conversation as we walk back towards his car. "I'll be in touch," he says, giving me a smile and a big thumbs up. I will process our whole conversation during my classes that afternoon. I really didn't get a chance to say anything. After my last class, I return to my office and notice Big Papa has called my cell, so I call him back.

He sounds excited. "How did it go?"

"Great," I say. "I think. Roger said he'll help me raise $100,000."

"Yes, he said the same when I talked to him. He also said, *if I'm stuck in a foxhole, that's the guy I want in there with me.*"

"He did not say that."

"He did, indeed. But you don't sound so thrilled."

I tell him I'm just tired after a long teaching day.

"Rest up, professor. See you in Pine Plains this weekend. You did great today."

Shouldn't I feel great? After all, someone just told me they want to raise a ton of money to support my campaign. I know I should be elated and grateful. But why do I feel as if my troubles have just begun?

The four countywide candidates have our coming out party at the Stissing Center in Pine Plains, which is a little town on the northern edge of the county. The place is packed with curious Democrats and NOPs converging on this theatre from all over northern Dutchess to get a good look at this new batch of 2023 hopefuls. It's been a while since I've spent time up here, and I'm impressed with how much this rural corner of Dutchess has changed -- for the better, in my humble opinion. Take Pine Plains, for instance. Driving through this one-stoplight town ten years ago, I'd witness a 1970s time warp of redneck farmers and a few old hippies in rusty Chevy pickups with *WALL DRUG* and *Keep On Truckin'*

bumper stickers. Today, I see a lot of family SUVs with rainbow stickers and soccer ball decals in the rear window. I'd heard the rumor that a lot of young folks had moved up to this area from Brooklyn during COVID, but this is the first time I'm seeing the evidence first-hand. That's promising news for Democrats trying to turn the county blue. Sure, there are still plenty of old hippies at the forum today, but I'm also meeting a solid number of younger residents, which is a nice surprise. One of them turns out to be Chris Drago, who was raised here and will be challenging the longtime Republican county legislator this year for this district. Wonderful story! There's more on Chris later in the book.

Today's plan at the Stissing Center is to put Anthony, Jim, Kenya and me on stage to introduce ourselves, answer some canned questions from Big Papa, and then end with some audience Q&A. The only part I'm nervous about is the Q&A; I think I proved I can get a crowd up and moving back at the county convention – *good trouble!* – but that's not helpful when someone asks you a question you can't answer. I am about to learn a valuable lesson: "winging it" can only take me so far. When it comes to the important issues, I need to do my homework. I need to become bulletproof, prepared for any question that comes my way. It's the end of March, and my platform is still very much a work in progress. Today in Pine Plains, I'm worried about getting questions I can't answer, simply because I don't know enough. As the saying goes, you don't get a second chance at a first impression. Later in the campaign, I will turn that weakness into a strength. But today in Pine Plains, I am going to take my lumps. A lot of them.

All four of us are obviously shaking off rust at the start of the event. Some of us stand up to answer the questions, some remain sitting. This is our first time sharing a stage together, and it's clear we're not working as a team yet. But hey, we have to start somewhere. We all have different strengths, but we also have different things to work on, too. For example, Kenya and I are already accomplished public speakers; in fact, from this point on, whenever the four of us speak at an event we will invoke the Kenya Rule – that is, don't ever be the person who has to speak AFTER Kenya Gadsden. (Yes, she is that good with the mic.) And while Anthony and Jim don't have the same speaking skills yet they bring a wealth of knowledge that I simply don't have. With 25 years of work as a prosecutor, Anthony Parisi knows more than just about anyone how the legal system works in Dutchess County. Whenever he speaks today, he's using legal terms and acronyms I've never heard before, like he's speaking a different language. And Jim Rogers might lack laser focus when he's speaking – but whoa, this guy really knows how the Family Court system works (or doesn't work, in this case.) Sitting here on stage, I have to say, I am in awe of all three of my new teammates.

We get to the dreaded Q&A and just as I'd feared, I'm getting most of the questions. Someone asks me what I plan to do about the housing crisis. Someone else asks me why the county bus service is so bad up here in northern Dutchess. I do my best to answer, but I can feel myself sputtering and going in circles. When Anthony gets a question about crime rates, it's right in his wheelhouse and he responds with a series of facts and a specific plan to reduce crime in the county. It's beautiful to listen to but it just makes me feel more of a failure in comparison. I'm still just a snake oil salesman. Then a woman in the back row I've never met before asks me the Kobayashi Maru.

"This question is for Tommy," she says, both hands cradling the microphone. "The county budget is around $350 million each year. How can I trust you with all that money?"

You don't have to be a Star Trek fan to know the Kobayashi Maru. It's a simulator test at Star Fleet Academy where a fictional cargo ship named the Kobayashi Maru is sending out a distress signal from the no-go Neutral Zone. If you choose to rescue the ship, you die. If you choose not to rescue the drifting ship, they die. Damned if you do, damned if you don't. Then a young cadet named James T. Kirk cheats by reprogramming the simulation and becomes the only one to ever pass the Kobayashi Maru test. (How he didn't get expelled, I have no idea. I'm more of a Star Wars guy, myself.) Today, I don't have the option to change the rules. I am being stared down by a woman who has probably been disappointed by every previous Democrat candidate for County Executive over the last 32 years. She's not a Republican plant asking an impossible question to trip me up, she's just a county resident who is sick and tired of the same canned questions, and the same robot-like responses. And I don't want to let her down. There's no correct answer to her question, of course; I can't prove to her on the spot I am trustworthy. That's probably why she asked it; she wants to see what kind of stuff I'm made of. Luckily, I'm a quick learner. And one of the first lessons I've learned so far during my initiation on the campaign trail is, don't answer a question you don't want to be asked. Instead, answer the question you *want* to be asked.

"That's a great question," I say, stalling for a moment to gather my thoughts. "But I think what you're really asking is, why can't we trust the county government we have now? I mean, how many people here today are sick and tired of the back door deals, like $25 million of your taxpayer money going to improve a baseball stadium while you can't even get EMS services up here in northern Dutchess?" That one hit a nerve; now the entire room is grumbling. That reaction allows me to stall a few moments more; I acknowledge the discontent in the room by shaking my head in disgust right along with them.

Everyone in Dutchess County has heard this story, and most are still hot about it. Last year, the current county government passed a last-minute bill, without any outside input or discussion, to give $25 million of county funds to make luxury renovations to Dutchess County Stadium, the home of the Hudson Valley Renegades, a minor league ball club for the New York Yankees.

That's a lot of money for even NYC, much less a half-rural upstate county like Dutchess. And it's not a good look for Republicans when we have so many issues that desperately could have used those funds. People are pissed.

After the grumbling dies down, I turn back to the woman. "Honestly ma'am, I can't convince you today that you can trust me with your hard-earned money," I say, making eye contact with her. "I'm not going to make you promises when it's clear everyone is tired of the same old campaign promises, year after year. But I sure as hell hope you'll trust me more than the people who would rather give $25 million of your money to the New York Yankees instead of delivering the vital services you deserve." That did it. Voices are breaking out all over the place with opinions about the stadium debacle. The room gets so loud that Big Papa has to grab the mic and call for order. There's some applause, too, which makes me feel good, but with all the noise I'm still focused on this one woman's reaction. We're still making eye contact when she finally nods her head, cracks a warm smile and says, "Thank you for answering my question."

Somehow, I managed to pass my first Kobayashi Maru test. (Eat your heart out, Captain Kirk.) But it still doesn't make up for the fact that I didn't do very well at this candidate forum, overall. Today I learned that being an engaging speaker is a valuable skill, sure, but a good candidate must do more than that. Voters want substance, too. They want to trust I know what I'm doing, and right now it's obvious that I don't. Fortunately, I will have a lot more events like this one in the months ahead, and I will get much better. March is about to end. In a way, the month has served as a sort of gatekeeper as I keep descending deeper into this world of local politics. I'd say I passed the initiation, but barely. The professor in me would give my efforts a solid C+. I know I simply have to do better. But I also know the learning curve will only get steeper from here.

THIRD CIRCLE

Go Tommy, it's your birthday! For the last seven years or so, I've held a fundraiser for veterans on my birthday in early April. It started out as a modest idea – thirty friends or so at the VFW, rocking out to my reunited rock band from fat camp, the Stretch Marks (no, that is not a typo) – I think we raised a little over a thousand bucks back then. But with the fifteen minutes of fame that came with walking across the country, my birthday event has grown so big we had to move it from the VFW to Mahoney's on the Poughkeepsie waterfront. These days we raise funds for VetZero, the nonprofit I created with Christa after the walk – but this year it's about kicking off the campaign, so we're not raising funds at all. I've invited my countywide teammates as well as Yvette to bring their people, and together with my usual mob and some curious strangers, we've managed to pack the place. Standing room only. There's plenty of kids here, too, which is a refreshing change from the stuffy cheese-and-cracker campaign events I've ever attended. But that's the point, right? The theme of the event is "We Are Family" because I want people to know this campaign is going to feel different from the start. It's not going to feel like a political campaign. It's going to feel like family.

Amelia and Big Papa are skeptical when I originally told them about my birthday event. They've probably helped organize hundreds of campaign events between them, but I'm guessing none of them involved birthday cake with sprinkles, fun activities for the kids, or a t-shirt giveaway. (Shoot! I haven't told them about the TEAM TOMMY shirts I'm giving out on my birthday.) Nora designed them and we used a local, family-run business to make them. They look great!

"Come on, Tommy," Amelia says with a sigh. "Don't waste your money on t-shirts."

Big Papa doesn't seem to care much about the shirts, but he has a lot of questions about the birthday itself. "Who is going to MC the event?"

"I am," I say, pausing like this is a trick question. "It's my *birthday*."

He waves his hand. "Oh, no. You can't MC your own event," he says, turning to Amelia. "Who do we know who could do it on short notice?"

Amelia thinks for a moment and rattles off a few names I've never heard before. "How about Linda from Beacon?"

Big Papa rubs his chin. "I agree, Linda would do a great job. Or maybe –"

"Guys, I'm standing *right here*," I say, interrupting their conversation. "This is my event. I do it every year. Trust me, it'll be great."

And it does turn out to be great. We planned for about 100 people to show up, but we stopped counting at 150. Democrat VIPs like Congressman Pat Ryan and Assemblyman Jonathan Jacobson stop by to see what all the commotion is about. Even better, there's a wonderful energy in the room because people are actually having a blast, complete with a dozen or so kids running around. It feels more like a family reunion in here than some stuffy campaign kickoff. All the countywide speeches are great from Anthony, Jim, Kenya and Yvette, and Kenya even sings *Happy Birthday* to me from the podium. You can't beat that! This might, in fact, be my favorite birthday ever – there might be competition from my eighth birthday when we played Pin the Tail on Godzilla and ate a Carvel ice cream cake (Fudgie the Whale – hey, if you know, you know.)

As people begin to leave, Big Papa comes over while I'm finally getting a moment to myself to enjoy a piece of birthday cake. He puts a gentle hand on my shoulder. "I might have misjudged you," he says. "This was amazing. There were so many people I've never seen before." He's clearly impressed, which is a big leap from our first meeting back in February at the sad café when he pegged me as an introverted English professor. What he doesn't know is that I have always been an introvert, even as a kid. And I've spent my 54 years of life trying to find ways to compensate – and often over-compensate – for the crippling shyness only true introverts can understand.

When I was a younger man, my Dad gave me some honest advice I still hold in my heart today. Basically, he said never count on being the smartest person in the room. Never count on being the most talented, the most charismatic, the most creative, or the most outgoing either, because you probably won't be. But you can always choose to be the hardest working person in the room. You can always be the person who shows up early and stays until the job is done. And that consistent work ethic can open doors for you that frankly, all those other qualities simply cannot.

Always show up, he taught me. When you show up, good things will happen. It's the same lesson psychologist Angela Duckworth would famously convey in her 2016 bestselling book *Grit*. "Talent counts," she writes. "But effort counts twice." Looking back now, I can see my Dad was trying to teach me the secret of hard work; if you're doing something you love, the old saying goes, you'll never work a day in your life. He took up the sport of judo in his 40s as a way to stay in shape and into his 70s, he was competing for medals at the Judo World Championships against much younger men.

This is also the guy who built his own sawmill so he could mill his own boards as he learned the craft of woodworking.

If you truly want to do something, do it. Commit to it, and never look back.

Listen, I could never compete in judo or build my own woodworking shop and frankly, I would never want to try. Not my thing. But I have managed to write five books and walk across America alone without being eaten by mountain lions. It's become a defense mechanism, really: *when in doubt, just work harder*. And that motor has been a blessing so many times in life, helping me break free of my shyness more times than I can count. But sometimes it's been a curse, too. For example, try having a meaningful relationship with a guy who is always percolating a dozen different ideas in his head on how to make the world a better place – serving veterans, housing the homeless, defending survivors of domestic violence, feeding hungry kids, and so on. Once you start that motor, I guess it's hard to turn it off again. I'll admit having a voice in my head 24/7 that keeps whispering *do more, do more, do more*. (The Fiancée is reading this part right now and saying, *No shit, Sherlock*.) But I'm hoping that relentless energy proves to be my secret weapon when I hit the campaign trail full-on, starting in May.

A famous poet once said, April is the cruelest month. Was that Shakespeare? T.S. Eliot? Wu Tang Clan? Whoever came up with that bit of wisdom, there's a good chance they were running for office at the time. Sure, conventional wisdom tells us the very end of a campaign would be the cruelest time – early November, when everything comes down to the wire. But that's the most exciting time too, when the adrenaline is pumping hardest as everyone comes together for the final push. Besides, *November is the*

cruelest month just doesn't have the same ring to it – and excuse me, Thanksgiving? Grandma's stuffing, with the burnt edges? Pumpkin pie? Heck, *any* kind of pie is the opposite of cruelty. The defense rests, your honor. No, ask anybody who has run for serious office about their least favorite time during their campaign, and they will likely say April and early May. Ask them why, and I guarantee every candidate will shudder before they whisper the same two words, slowly, with a snarl.

Call Time.

If there is one element of a political campaign that deserves its very own Circle of Hell, it's call time. Or dialing for dollars, as my friend Jack calls it. Call time is the act of cold-calling potential donors and trying to engage them before they hang up, or worse. It's worse than being a telemarketer, because at least when you are telemarketing, you're selling a product you don't have to care much about. When you are doing call time for your campaign, however, you are selling yourself. And there is nothing that sucks the marrow out of your soul more than having to sell yourself to complete strangers in thirty or forty phone calls at a time, five days a week.

Big Papa has hooked us up with a big-time New York PR firm that specializes in political campaigns. We picked them because of their track record: they were the firm that helped Michelle Hinchey defeat Sue Serino in last year's race for state senate. After a couple of Zoom calls, though, it's clear we can't afford any of the services they offer right now; not without some fundraising help, anyway. (Counting on you, Roger Devereaux.) But in the meantime, they do connect me with a NYC fundraising guy named Cillian who seems cheery on the phone and agrees to make the two-hour drive up from the city so he can give me a crash course in all things fundraising – including the dreaded call time.

We meet in the late afternoon at the same law office where I met Amelia and big Papa back in February. The office is located on the busy one-way arterial that runs through the middle of Poughkeepsie; during rush hour, the traffic whizzes by so fast you have to say a little prayer before turning into the parking lot, hoping no one rear-ends you. Cillian lives in Manhattan, so I figure he's used to it. He's a good-looking, gangly young man in his twenties wearing a blazer and an iPad case slung over his shoulder. We go over some of the basics on how call time works. We'll pay his firm a flat fee for each call list of potential donors they provide, one at a time. The lists are filled with the contact info of people who have donated to Democrat candidates in the past; most donors will live locally in the Hudson Valley, but some of the bigger names will be in New York City. Every name on the call list will have a suggested ask amount next to it – that is, a dollar amount they have given previously to a candidate. My lists will be ordered by the ask amount, in descending order, starting with $5000 and moving down to $100. "April and May are the best time to start your call time, because the kids are still in school and people are still home," Cillian says. "When summer comes, good luck getting in touch with anybody. Nobody picks up the phone when they're on the beach in Nantucket. It'll be end of August before you can call them again."

"That makes sense," I say.

"It's already April, so I think you should start right away. Do you have your cell on you?"

"Sure do," I say, laying it on the table between us. It's an oldie, but a goodie.

"First, I'm going to have you download an app that will transfer all your contacts to a spreadsheet that you can use as your first call list."

I look down at my phone. "You want to download my contacts?"

"Yes, we call it *rolodexing*. You start with all the people you are already connected with, so it's easier than just cold calling." I'm not sure this kid is old enough to have ever seen an actual rolodex in the wild, but that's not the problem. "Now, how many contacts do you have in your phone?"

Ah. There's the problem. "I think I have twelve? Give or take." I open the contact list on my phone and do a quick count. "No, I was wrong. Eleven."

He is genuinely shocked. "You're joking, right?"

I turn my screen around to show him that I am not joking. I realize he's used to dealing with seasoned candidates from NYC who could probably rolodex a thousand contacts off their phone in a heartbeat, not a middle-aged English professor from Poughkeepsie who only keeps the numbers he needs to call, which are: (1) Yonkers, (2) the Cabin, (3) Capricorn, (4) Johnny Z, (5) CEO, (6) the Fiancée, (7) Mickey, (8) Ted, (9) Nora, (10) Nate the Great, and (11) Uncle Robert. That's all. Wait, Yonkers and the Cabin are both really my Dad, so I guess we're down to ten. Cillian stares at me like he's an archaeologist who just uncovered a new kind of dinosaur. I'm sure he can't wait to get back to the office and tell everyone about the guy running for Dutchess County Executive with ten contacts in his phone. I imagine reactions of both panic and sadness. "How does he live?" one will say, shaking their head in bewilderment.

The horror, the horror.

It's clear the rolodexing thing is not going to be super-useful today, so we wrap up after talking about call time. "I'll get working on your first call lists tonight, so you can start making calls by the end of the week," he says with confidence. We agree to do a trial run together on Zoom, where he can watch me make some calls and give me some notes. That should be fun. By the time we exit the building it's dark outside, with the usual three-lane murder of commuter traffic flying past on the arterial towards the Mid-Hudson Bridge. Cillian gets into his BMW and – to my horror – makes a right turn, heading directly into oncoming traffic on the one-way arterial. I shout at the top of my lungs for him to stop, but he can't hear me. His taillights disappear down the dark street going in the wrong direction. A second later I hear angry car horns blaring, but thankfully I don't hear a crash. I'm hoping he managed to veer off onto a side street before he got into an accident, or worse, gets pulled out of his sports car and pummeled by a furious swarm of locals trying to get home for *Wheel of Fortune*. This is Poughkeepsie, after all. Our priorities might be different than the rest of the country.

Turns out, I needn't worry because a week later it's me, Ted, and Cillian on the Zoom call and I don't see any bandages or bruises on the kid's face. I make a dozen calls on my cell as they watch, which feels weird, like I'm back in college taking an exam with a proctor looking over my shoulder. I have a brief pitch written down in front of me to start each call – *Hi [First Name] this is Tommy Zurhellen. How are you? I'm the Democrat running for Dutchess County Executive this year. Do you have a minute?* – that is, if they pick up. Turns out, it's a big if, because I go straight to voice mail on half the calls. "You're going to get a lot of those," Cillian says. "People don't pick up as much as they used to."

But it's not all bad news on my first call time. I do manage to engage a few people enough to get two donation pledges and one actual donation on the spot. They're small, but it's better than nothing. "You're a natural," Cillian says. Ted has the unenviable job of logging updated info on the call lists each week, so we can keep track of the yesses, the maybes, and the *oh, hell nos*. After an hour of logging calls, I feel like I'm getting the hang of it.

"How much call time should I be doing?" I ask Cillian.

"With your fundraising goal, you should aim for 20 hours a week," he says, tapping his iPad a few times. "I know that sounds like a lot, but you're already behind. You need to catch up. Weekday afternoons are best. But stay away from Fridays. You can do it!"

After Cillian logs off, Ted and I stay on the Zoom for a few minutes to talk. "Twenty hours a week?" I say.

"Yeah," Ted says. "And you teach weekday afternoons, right?"

"All except Fridays," I say. "But I'm not supposed to call on Fridays."

"Perfect," he says. "At least you're a natural."

My teaching schedule at Marist is going to limit my ability to get out and hit the campaign trail until the second week of May, when the semester ends. But it's not a huge loss at this point, because all the important public events for candidates – the farmer's markets, county picnics, street fairs, and so on – don't start until mid-May anyway. But we've still got a lot of busy work to do in April, starting with petitioning for signatures to get our candidates on the ballot. When your party nominates you as their official candidate, you still must collect a prescribed number of signatures from registered voters in your party. For the four countywide candidates, it's up to each local committee to get out and knock on doors in their town to get enough signatures to get a candidate on the ballot. To be safe, you want to collect *double* the number of signatures required, especially if you're a Democrat – part of the Republican playbook in Dutchess County is to automatically challenge their opponents' signatures in court, hoping they luck out and find a technicality to get some signatures disqualified. If you're a candidate for more than one party, you have to get signatures for each; for example, I'm the Democrat for Dutchess County Executive this year but I'm also the Working Families Party candidate at the same time, which is a common pairing.

Big Papa is happy because by the end of April, all the countywide candidates have well over twice the signatures needed. I hear it's a record, which feels good. All that's left to do is scrub and compile the lists and deliver them to the county board of elections in Poughkeepsie.

Third Circle

Even though I'm busy with school and all this busy work in April, I'm still finding time to attend events in the community, especially veteran events. Since the walk, I've gained a formidable reputation as a veterans' advocate, so as you might imagine I receive a lot of invitations to stuff. There's one event I definitely don't want to miss this month, a press conference at the VA with Senator Kirsten Gillibrand. She's trying to get the word out to veterans about the PACT Act, a groundbreaking new law that expands healthcare for veterans who were exposed to toxic chemicals from sources like burn pits during their military service. It means millions of veterans who were not eligible for healthcare from the VA are now eligible – and that includes me. So, I'm not here as a candidate or a fellow Democrat, I'm here as a veteran who knows how vital the PACT Act is going to be in the years to come. Okay, I'm also here as a fan – not only is Senator Gillibrand a chief architect of the PACT Act, she's also a key proponent for funding the HUD-VASH program, which supplies housing vouchers to homeless veterans. Yes, I do my homework when it comes to supporting veterans. Senator Gillibrand walks the walk when it comes to our heroes, and that makes her a hero in my book, too.

The Senator is late, but I know the press conference will go quickly. As we wait, there's a big group of local veterans gathered on one side of the room, jawing and laughing. On the other side, there's a gaggle of politicians and aides staring quietly into their phones, including folks like Amelia and Jonathan.

Guess which group I'm standing with.

Senator Gillibrand delivers some remarks and after the press conference is over, they set up a receiving line so people can take a photo with the Senator. As you already know, I don't like photo-ops in general, but I especially don't like them when veterans are involved. So, I stay in the back corner of the room, catching up with veterans I know. Amelia is standing up at the podium next to the Senator, giving an introduction of each person in line if it's needed. She sees me hanging out in the back of the room and tilts her head as if to say, *get in the line.* When I don't, she comes over. "You need to get in line and take a picture with the Senator."

"Do I really?" I probably sound like a kid who spent too much time in the pool.

She crosses her arms. "Yes. You need to take advantage of opportunities like this."

Okay, she has a point. So, I step into the receiving line, waiting patiently for my turn. At least I get to shake hands with someone I truly admire. When I get to the front of the line, Amelia starts to tell the Senator who I am – but to my surprise, the intro isn't really necessary.

"Hey, I know you," Senator Gillibrand says, reaching out her hand. "You're the guy who walked across America." As we take our photo, she asks me about the walk (she's an avid walker herself) and my time in the Navy. She could not be nicer, or more genuine. But in no time, we're interrupted by her handlers who are trying to keep things moving.

"Good luck with your campaign," the Senator says. "Keep walking."

They say never meet your heroes. But today I'm making an exception to that rule.

My first two weeks of call time are bumpy at best. There's nothing an introvert loves more than to cold-call strangers while they're having dinner and asking them for money. I'm not very good at it, but in my defense, I will say I am doing my best. Carving out time around between my classes is tough, and it's abundantly clear I'm not going to get close to those 20 hours per week Cillian was talking about, at least while school is still in session. I can log 20-30 calls in two hours, depending on how many people pick up.

To start, I try building my confidence with some easy calls, so I look at the list for any names I know. Bingo: I see my old friend Wendy on the call list of Democrat donors, so I dial the number and after a few rings, she picks up. "Hello?"

"Hey, Wendy, it's Tommy Zurhellen." I sound way too chipper, like a game show host. "How are you today?"

"Hi, Tommy." Her voice sounds sad, like she's about to cry. Then I realize she's been expecting my call. I don't have a chance to dig into the script before she starts talking. "I have to tell you, Tommy, I'm torn. I'm a Democrat through and through. But I'll never forget when my mother was sick, Sue called me. That goes a long way in my book. She called me right up, can you believe that?"

"Well, I'm calling you now," I say, scrambling to get back to the script. "I know you care about issues like…"

"Like I said, Tommy. I'm torn." And then she hangs up.

So much for easy. I don't see a category for "torn" on the call sheet, so I just mark the call as a maybe. After all, Wendy didn't actually say no.

I wish I could tell you it gets better from here. On the bright side, school will be over soon and in a couple weeks I'll be able to get out on the campaign trail and do my thing.

FOURTH CIRCLE

MAY BEGINS with a sordid scandal that absolutely rocks the veteran community in the Hudson Valley and far beyond. A local veteran advocate has reported that twenty homeless veterans were kicked out of a hotel to make way for migrants sent up from New York City seeking temporary housing. The story instantly causes an uproar and quickly goes viral, getting picked up by media outlets nationwide. The issue of migrants being bussed up from NYC is already a hot topic, but this announcement throws a truckload of gasoline onto the fire. And as you might expect, just about every politician in the Hudson Valley – including my good friend Pat Ryan, a veteran himself -- immediately jumps on their soapbox to condemn this horrible act. They are all looking for blood.

Well, all except one.

"Are you going to put out a press release on this?" Ted asks for the third time in two days. He's nervous. "I'm getting a lot of calls. Everyone's been asking why you haven't said anything publicly about it yet."

I know, because I'm getting the same calls. My phone is filled with prickly messages asking why I haven't joined the chorus, especially since I'm a veteran myself. One person asks if I even care about veterans, which hurts. "Your silence is saying a lot," another person says, which hurts even more. But I don't respond, and I definitely don't send out a press release. You see, I have been working in the local veteran community for years now, and I know something these other folks don't know.

I know the story is probably a complete lie.

The veteran community in the Hudson Valley is a tight-knit group. All the various veteran advocacy organizations meet once a week on Zoom as part of our Hudson Valley Veterans Task Force (HVVTF) to share information and resources. We all know each other on a first-name basis; we also know exactly who does what when it comes to helping veterans: housing, transportation, mental health, you name it. We know how many homeless veterans, both housed and unhoused, are currently living in each county because there are agencies who track that information. It's what they do. So, when the veterans advocate in question suddenly announces that the veterans they were housing in a hotel were put out on the street, anyone in the HVVTF automatically knows that's probably bullshit.

And indeed, the entire story turns out to be bullshit. The whole story is fabricated. It only takes a few days for reporters to discover the hotel had never heard of the advocate and had never housed homeless veterans. And the displaced "veterans" turned out to be not veterans at all; they were homeless men who were paid to pretend to act as veterans. Why would someone perpetrate such a hoax? Hey, that's above my pay grade. But I will say I have crossed paths before with this local advocate who created this whole mess. They are a veteran who served in Iraq, and if this was just another book about politics, I'd probably spend time going down the wormhole and "exposing" all their deceitful actions. But this is a book about kindness, so instead I will simply say as a fellow veteran to another, I hope they receive the mental health support they obviously need. I'm not even going to use their name in this book, because I figure they have enough problems ahead.

Besides, the whole sad affair can be found easily on the internet. One year later in 2024, we will learn that they have been charged by the FBI for stolen valor and other federal crimes that could add up to 20 years in prison. So, I don't think anyone needs to pour more gasoline on that fire.

But a veteran concocting this fake story is not the worst part of the scandal. Not by a long shot. The worst part, the part that can't be easily scrubbed away, belongs to all the politicians who didn't do their homework and suddenly have amnesia when the story turns out to be false. Most of these people will never apologize for their own reckless behavior in stoking the flames before they even verified if the story is true, or not. (To his credit, Congressman Pat Ryan did make a public apology.) Others simply point their fingers at the veterans advocate who duped them, or worse, they say nothing at all, hoping the scandal will quietly pass. But the damage has already been done. They don't realize the integrity of our veteran community is diminished every time politicians blow up a story like this one, and then simply walk away when the story isn't true. To me, that is the definition of cowardice. And as we will see later in this chapter, cowardice can be downright dangerous, because people will still think the story of veterans being displaced by migrants is true, even though it is not.

I will never receive apologies from any of those folks who left messages questioning my commitment to helping veterans, but that's okay. They probably had good intentions, after all. But this whole experience at the start of May has taught me a couple of valuable lessons that I will take with me on the campaign trail ahead. First, I'm going to do a better job trusting my own instincts, which might get me into trouble when I don't trust the advice of others as much. I have to give myself permission to be patient and work things out on my own, even when the world is flying past so quickly. I have to trust all the things that brought me to this point – everything in my weird and wonderful life so far, from the Navy to the walk across America, and all the bizarre stories in between – have given me the experiences I need to navigate any challenge ahead.

In other words, I know stuff. I'm not a fool who thinks he knows everything, of course. But I probably know things others do not.

Second, I'm not going to be afraid to do things my way. When the phone is ringing off the hook with people saying you're doing it wrong, it takes a lot of old-fashioned gumption to stay the course under all that pressure. I need to be true to myself and always remember this journey is called *The High Road* for a reason. This is a journey about kindness, not fear. Otherwise, what's the point? Maya Angelou once said, "It takes courage to be kind." I truly believe that, and I'm slowly learning that I'll have to find the courage to stay on the path of kindness, even when people around me want to push me off. That's no easy task. I'm going to get plenty more angry calls in the months ahead. But the alternative to courage is cowardice, and I think we've already established there's no way in Hell I'm ever doing that.

Speaking of blowing up my phone, Jonathan Jacobson has been calling nonstop lately, trying to set up a Zoom meeting so he can give me advice on my campaign. He's the Assemblyman for southern Dutchess and a chunk of Orange County across the river, including Newburgh. Jonathan is what I would call an "old-school" politician. For starters, he's always wearing a blazer and a name tag. I've noticed he shows up to every event, including my birthday. He doesn't seem to trust social media much, though. He is slender and soft-spoken. Basically, he appears to be the exact opposite of a guy like me. But I'll tell you right now, don't sleep on Jonathan Jacobson. There's a reason why Republicans have stopped trying to run a candidate against him. It's because he gets results. He's always bringing back funds from Albany for businesses and nonprofits in his district – he might hold the world record for number of times presenting the "big check" to folks. So, I have a lot of respect for Jonathan. At the same time, I'm not sure if he holds much respect for me in return; he probably just sees this big, sloppy guy with a big mouth and bad hair who's doing everything wrong. So, I suspect this meeting is supposed to be some kind of coachable moment.

Oh, goody.

Ted and I finally connect with Jonathan on a three-way Zoom one afternoon. Jonathan is sitting behind his desk in his Newburgh office. And yes, he is wearing a blazer. And a nametag. "You've got to read the newspapers," he starts off saying. "You know, keep up on current events." Which sounds like great advice – if I was running for office in 1975. But I don't say anything.

Then he gets to the good stuff. "You need to wear a nametag everywhere you go, okay? Do you have a nametag? I have a great nametag guy if you don't."

"I'm not wearing a nametag," I say. Whoa! Who is *this* guy, saying what he feels out loud? I can see Ted raising his eyebrow.

Jonathan smiles. "But you've got to wear a nametag. No one knows who you are."

I don't agree with that last one, but I also don't want to argue. I rap my knuckles on my desk. "What else you got, Jonathan?"

He seems shaken, as if the coachable moment he envisioned has already gone sour. "All right," he says. "What kind of events are you attending?"

Ted rattles off a few of the community events I've hit so far.

"*Those events don't matter,*" Jonathan says emphatically. I've never heard him raise his voice before. He then proceeds to tell us the kind of events I should be attending; I hope Ted is writing them down because to be honest I've stopped listening. The rest of the call doesn't get much better as Jonathan rattles off other things I should be doing. "Well, I guess that's all," he says with a tired sigh before he signs off.

I lean back in my chair for a moment. Why am I so riled up right now?

"You were pretty harsh on him, Cuz," Ted says.

Ted's right, of course. And I do feel bad. But I'd rather be straight now with Jonathan and the other folks trying to steer me this way or that, rather than disappoint them later. Look, one person calls to tell me I should be spending my time knocking on doors, while at the same time another says I should only be doing call time. I'm tired of being pushed around. I'm tired of the disorganization. And I think my frustration being stuck in the middle of this windstorm for the last couple months overflowed on the call with Jonathan.

Listen, I'm not wearing a nametag. I'm not showing up at events just because they are "target-rich" with the most registered voters; I'm showing up at the events I'm passionate about, where I have a chance to learn something new. All this probably sounds ridiculous to a career politician like Jonathan who clearly follows the old-school campaign playbook on how to win elections. But I'm not a career politician, and I'm not going through this journey just to win some election. I'm doing it because I want to help people. And I think that's the difference. Win or lose, I never want to look in the mirror and see a politician staring back. I don't want to ever see a guy who pounces on a scandal because it's the smart political move. I just want to look in the mirror and see me.

I'm finally done with the spring semester at Marist (everyone passed!) so now I can get out on the campaign trail full-time and visit as many events as I can. To start, Ted and I are ambitious in finding every firehouse barbecue, farm tour, block party, and everything in between. Well, maybe we are too ambitious. Some days I will fit as many as seven or eight different events into my schedule, but a lot of the events are a waste of time, at least at the beginning. For example, one day I visit a llama farm and then stop by a brewery to listen to the MAGA-friendly owner pontificate for an hour about the homeless and drug addicts. Not the best use of my time. But we slowly will get better at choosing events. Over the course of the summer, my teammate Kenya will often talk about "the two Tommys." That is, there must be *two* Tommy Zurhellens running around the county because there's no way one guy could be hitting all those events.

As the weather warms up, farmers' markets start popping up like wildflowers in towns across Dutchess County, from Millerton to Beacon. For locals and weekenders from NYC alike, it's a great way to get fresh produce, support local businesses and keep the kids occupied when they're not at soccer or swim practice. But for candidates like me, the farmer's market circuit is a campaign trail staple for meeting new people and talking to small business owners. There's only one catch: most market co-ops are nonprofit organizations, which means they don't allow candidates to actively campaign. That means no buttons or nametags – which suits me just fine, actually. With practice, I'm getting better at engaging people I meet walking the stalls, and I'm not nearly as discouraged when people ignore or dismiss me. It's all part of the job.

It's Saturday morning which means my first stop of the day is the Hyde Park Farmer's Market. It's basically twenty or so pop-up tents lined up in a lumpy gravel lot across from the library. There used to be a car dealership here. Most of the vendors are here week after week, so I know most of them already. Others I know to avoid; Sue Serino lives in Hyde Park after all, and Serino Realty is located directly across the street from this gravel lot. She's got all her lawn signs stacked on the sidewalk – GO SUE GO! and WOMEN FOR SUE! as well as my personal favorite VETS FOR SERINO – so the place is hard to miss. Talk about walking into the Lion's Den! But even though I'm in enemy territory I always find a way to meet new folks here, and besides, I usually walk away with a plastic bag stuffed with fresh veggies along with fantastic baked goods made with love by my friends at Little Loaf Bakery. They make this pretzel-croissant thing with an olive tapenade I simply can't resist. There's also a die-hard hippie couple (Democrats, naturally) selling exotic mushrooms from their backyard garden who I love talking with each week.

No, not *those* kinds of mushrooms.

Today I'm doing a slow lap around the stalls this morning and I've just left the mushroom couple when a woman approaches me wearing an official-looking Hyde Park Farmer's Market t-shirt. I assume she's in charge. Her face looks vaguely familiar; it's clear she knows who I am. "Excuse me," she says. "You're not campaigning here, are you?"

"No ma'am," I say, holding up my bag of goodies. "See? No name tag."

"I see. But you know that you're not allowed to campaign here, right?"

"I do know that. Thank you." Behind her in the back corner of the lot I can see an ambulance pulling up. "What happened there?" I say, pointing behind her.

"A lady slipped in the mud," she says. "Might've broken her leg. She should have been more careful." I'm about to ask if her time might be better spent tending to the wounded instead of harassing a guy with a bag of pastries and green beans, but it's clear she's not done with the interrogation quite yet. "So we're clear," she says, hands on her hips. "You know you're not allowed to campaign here."

I nod. "Let me ask you a question," I say, feeling a bit more feisty now. I look at my watch. "Was Sue here earlier?" This is a trick question. Thanks to social media, I know Sue's already been here and gone with her entourage.

"Why, yes she was," the woman says. "What does that matter?"

"I'm just wondering if you gave her the same line of questioning you're giving me."

This puts her on her heels for a moment, but she just laughs. "Oh, well. It's *Sue*," she says, as if describing a revered icon like a Pope or a President or Celine Dion. "I mean, everybody knows Sue."

"Don't I know it," I say. "Was she wearing a nametag?" Another trick question.

She smiles wanly. It's clear she's had enough of her own medicine because she starts walking backwards, towards the ambulance where EMS personnel are gently loading the poor woman who fell onto a gurney. "You just make sure you don't do any campaigning here," she says, waving a finger. "You've been warned."

It hasn't taken me long to figure out this won't be an even playing field as I run as the Democrat for Dutchess County Executive. Far from it. It's going to be an uphill battle all the way, and not just for me – all four of the countywide candidates are quickly realizing the weight of the Republicans' home-court advantage this year. Anthony Parisi, our candidate for District Attorney, is relating a gripping story on the campaign trail that perhaps sums it up best; I'll do my best to paraphrase his powerful anecdote here. Anthony has worked in the Dutchess DA's office for 25 years, and when he declared his candidacy for District Attorney, his boss Bill Grady – a Republican who has been DA here for 40 years -- brought Anthony into his office and demanded his resignation. Anthony asked why, and Grady told him it's going to be disruptive to the office. Then Anthony asked if Grady had asked his opponent to resign, since he also works in the same office. "No," Grady said, prompting Anthony to ask why not.

"Because you're a Democrat," Grady said, sticking a finger in Anthony's chest.

The story actually gets worse. When Anthony refused to resign, Grady asked him what he planned to do when both he and his wife (Sinead is also an attorney at the DA's office) are out of a job. Then

Fourth Circle

Bill Grady threatened Anthony's family; he asked how he expects to provide for his two young daughters when he's out on the street.

Absolutely despicable. Every time Anthony tells that story on the campaign trail, you can hear a pin drop in the room. All the countywide candidates have something at stake in this election, but for Anthony and Sinead, losing is simply not an option. If Kenya, Jim and I end up losing our races, we can always go back to our present jobs and find new ways to fight the good fight. If Anthony and Sinead lose this one, they're both fired. No wonder they're working harder than anyone, knocking on doors and even putting up their own billboards (nice carpentry skills, brother!) all over the county. I will hear Anthony tell that story maybe 100 times on the campaign trail this year – sometimes two or three times in the same day – but I have to tell you, it never gets old. It's a stark reminder that we all must work twice as hard if we want to have a chance to win. It's a dire warning that we're up against people who will do anything to stay on top of the mountain, including threatening a guy's family.

I've got my own uphill battle against former state senator Sue Serino. She's very well known around these parts, although she lost her senate re-election bid last year to Michelle Hinchey. Sue is regarded by virtually everyone as a nice person, including me – I've worked with her on veteran initiatives in the past, and she's always seemed pleasant to me. (And this book, like my campaign, is all about kindness, so I won't be visiting Negative Town here.) She already enjoys a home-court advantage with her name recognition, but the Republicans want to give her an even better head start in the race for County Executive, so as soon as Sue declared her candidacy back in February, they announced she was hired by the Dutchess County Office of the Aging to make phone calls to seniors. She will earn $43 dollars per hour. You read that right: the county hired my opponent to call voters during an election year.

And later this summer, news outlets will report Sue Serino has raised $250,000 for her campaign, a record. Talk about a head start! Big Papa was right, after all. Of course, no one will report how she raised that money, which comes mostly from corporate and PAC donations as well as funds left over from her failed senate bid last year. Spoiler alert: I will not raise $250,000 this year, or anything close to it. My donations average $25 and 100% are from individuals. I made it clear early on that I'm not accepting any corporate money – and heck, with this pro-union, anti-corruption campaign of kindness I'm running here, I highly doubt any corporation will come-a-courting anytime soon.

The news for Democrats isn't all bad this year. Thanks to COVID, a lot of people have moved up to Dutchess from Brooklyn over the last few years, particularly in northern Dutchess where it's more rural. That translates into roughly 20,000 more registered Democrats than Republicans now living in the county for 2023, which is a huge shift. The question is, will these people vote? Another advantage we have over our opponents this year is the use of social media. Anthony, Jim and Kenya are all up against old white guys who don't even have accounts on "the Facebook." My opponent Sue Serino is lucky to have my friend Carly as her campaign manager, so she is a couple steps above her teammates. But I have Nora, who is my secret weapon when it comes to getting the word out. The best part? Social media is largely free, so I can compete without selling my soul to corporations like the NRA and Central Hudson.

In politics, they say you either have the money, or the message. (I guess a campaign's goal is to have both.) But honestly, I don't really care about having the money. I'd much rather be the one with the message, because talking to folks about kindness and inclusion as I whip around the county with my teammates gives me the fuel I need. If I had a million bucks but I also had to defend wasteful spending or social injustice because people are paying me to do it, yikes – I would have quit a long time ago. Can you put a dollar amount on passion or a nonstop work ethic? How much is kindness worth in an election? I have no idea. But by the end of this thing, we're going to find out.

When Dante and Virgil arrive at the Fourth Circle of Hell, they discover a level of the underworld populated by those who committed the sins of avarice and greed – that is, the hoarders, the squanderers, and especially the wasteful spenders. The realm is guarded by Plutus, a classical deity of wealth. In writing the *Inferno*, it seems the poet Dante Alighieri had an especially frigid place in his heart for anyone who "spends without measure." Consider the grotesque fate of these souls in Canto VII as described by the character Dante himself:

> *I saw a nation of lost souls,*
> *Far more than in the circle above; they strained their chests*
> *Against huge bags of money, and with mad howls*
> *Pushed them at one another. Then in haste*
> *They pushed them back, one party shouting out,*
> *"Why do you hoard?" and the other, "Why do you waste?"*

A nation of lost souls, with two parties arguing endlessly over money? Whoa. Those lines were written 700 years ago in Italy about corrupt clergy, and yet they could easily pertain to American politics today. And in my case, they sure sound familiar as I hit the campaign trail as the Democrat for County Executive and start speaking out against the frankly shameful track record of the Republicans who have run Dutchess for the last 32 years.

Wasteful spending, indeed.

I've already mentioned the baseball stadium debacle in 2022, where the Republican super-majority in the Dutchess County Legislature agreed to give $25 million of county funds to make improvements at "the Dutch" aka Dutchess Stadium, to appease the New York Yankees' farm team. Did you know that at the same meeting, those same Republicans voted down Yvette Valdés Smith's proposal to make tuition free for county residents at our community college, which would cost a little over $500,000, or 1/50 of their gift to the Yankees? Yeah, shot down in flames. Their reasoning? "We don't have the money for that."

I don't think we don't need Allanis Morrisette to show us the irony here. We could use that $25 million to fight food insecurity, or stop poisoning our kids with lead pipes or fumes from the ancient trash incinerator, or a hundred other things to improve people's lives more than installing luxury boxes at a minor-league baseball park. And it certainly doesn't stop there. In late May I'm invited by a group of Pleasant Valley residents – Democrats and Republicans alike – to talk about a scandal I haven't even heard of yet. It seems the county purchased a property from the Boy Scouts located in Pleasant Valley called Camp Nooteeming for $5 million dollars last year. The County Executive at the time, Marc Molinaro, promised it would become a county park where kids could canoe and play soccer. But according to these town residents, that's not what happened at all. Instead, the county leased the property to an international corporation for a youth soccer training program, leaving locals angry because they're not able to use the property at all. Even worse, locals report there is music blaring from the PA system at odd hours of the night, and there are tractor trailers regularly speeding up and down the tiny access road, right past people's houses. "It's like the Indy 500 over there," one guy tells me at the meeting. "I want to wave a checkered flag as they pass by. I can't let my kids play in the road because it's way too dangerous." Other people at the meeting echo his frustration. Another resident says she complained to the County Executive's office numerous times, but the only answer she ever got was basically, *stop whining.*

These people are angry. They want someone to take their concerns seriously. So, when the meeting is over, the first thing I do is drive down the twisty country road to Camp Nooteeming, so I can see for myself. Sure enough, there's a big military-style gate and a scary sign at the entrance that reads NO TRESSPASSING. Wow. This is technically a county park, paid for with county funds, and yet no taxpayers are even allowed on the property? That's not leadership. That's not kindness. That's just cruelty.

I wish I could say these are the worst acts of wasteful spending perpetrated by the current county government, but that (dis)honor is reserved for the debate over the homeless shelter. Let me share some background. Up until COVID hit in 2020, Hudson River Housing (HRH) operated the county's emergency shelter for anyone experiencing homelessness for the past 40 years at a location called Webster House on the edge of Poughkeepsie. Webster served up to 60 people per night, give or take. But with COVID those numbers soared to 100 or even 150, and it was clear more space was needed to accommodate everyone who found themselves on the street. So, a temporary shelter was set up in an annex behind the Dutchess County Jail known as the PODs. HRH still operated the shelter with funds provided by the county. Now, flash forward three years: COVID has dissipated but there are still 100-150 clients staying in the shelter each night and the condition of the PODS has slowly deteriorated. I know all this because I've been on the Board of Directors at HRH since the walk, and besides, one of my best friends in the world is the CEO and President of HRH, Christa Hines. So yeah, you could say this one is personal for me. And for Christa, too.

Anyway, a replacement for the PODS needs to be found. So, the current County Executive Marc Molinaro and his allies on the County Legislature purchase property at 26 Oakley Street in

Poughkeepsie as the new shelter. They declare victory right away, but they should have done their homework instead before spending $3 million on the property because it's immediately apparent it could never serve as an effective shelter; there's not enough bedspace, not enough restroom facilities and worse, there's no kitchen facilities to heat meals. Under pressure, they reverse course and announce they are going to use the building at 26 Oakley Street as a legal annex, or a teaching annex, or something useful. That still leaves the question of where the county will house 100-150 people experiencing homelessness?

This is where the story gets worse. A lot worse.

The ultimate act of cruelty occurs when all the Republicans in the County Legislature – yes, all of them – vote to put the homeless people in the old jail. I was at this session, sitting in the gallery, when it happened. Dutchess County just spent $300 million to build a brand-new jail, right next to the old jail, which is located on Hamilton Street in the City of Poughkeepsie. Inmates will be moved over to the new jail as soon as it is completed, leaving the old jail empty. If you've ever driven by the old Dutchess County jail, then you already know what a scary place it is – and that's on the outside. And let's be clear: these legislators are not saying they want to renovate the facility before moving homeless folks in. They are saying, let's move the homeless folks in and *then* we will spend $1 million on a study to generate ideas on how to renovate the jail. Again, I was at the meeting when they agreed to this. Of course, Yvette and her entire Democrat caucus stood up and opposed the idea with fierce rhetoric, but it didn't matter. With the Republican super-majority in the Legislature, bad ideas get railroaded through all the time.

Whenever I get to the homeless shelter in my stump speech, I can hear the gasps from voters who have never heard this story before. They can't believe they live in a county where their elected leaders see nothing wrong with stuffing the homeless into jail cells. What if Dante Alighieri got a hold of a time machine from his neighbor Leonardo da Vinci and suddenly found himself in Dutchess County, New York in the year 2023? I imagine he'd go crazy for cell phones and soft-serve ice cream. But he would take one look at the avarice and wasteful spending, shake his head and say, "Più le cose cambiano, più rimangono le stesse!"

Or, the more things change, the more they stay the same!

Another good illustration of this tilted landscape my teammates and I are facing comes in the monumental, steel-cage street fight that future historians will undoubtedly refer to as the Great Dutchess County Office of the Aging Picnic Standoff of 2023. I'm joking, of course – in my humble opinion, the stakes could not be lower. We're talking about a picnic, after all. But don't tell the Dutchess Democrats that, because they are absolutely livid; this one might be the straw that broke the camel's back. Here's a summary of the sordid tale.

As we learned earlier in this chapter, our county government has an Office of the Aging which, besides allowing Sue Serino to call seniors and helping administer the Meals-on-Wheels program, has one job – to put on a series of summer picnics for seniors in every corner of Dutchess County. The picnics begin in late May and run until August, setting up a huge tent in a different town each week to serve a hot lunch and cold lemonade for an afternoon of food and fun. Hey, there's even a DJ playing sing-along hits from the 50s and 60s. Sounds harmless, doesn't it? Not entirely. You see, the picnics have also traditionally served as a wonderful campaign platform for Republicans in the county to get out the vote with seniors. Along with lunch, you'll also get to meet all your favorite incumbent politicians as they mill about with nametags and talk with the hundreds of seniors who show up at each picnic.

Talk about a captive audience. It's a racket for sure, and up until now Republicans haven't had to worry much about seeing undesirables – ahem, Democrats – show up to share the fun.

That is, until now.

The county sends out a cryptic memo a couple of weeks before the first picnic in late May. The memo announces a new rule this year, only seniors who live in that specific town will be allowed to access the picnic, along with (of course) county electeds and employees who work for the Office of the Aging. What a coincidence – my opponent now works for the Office of the Aging! Everyone else – including all the Democrat countywide candidates – are excluded. It's an idea straight out of the bag of dirty tricks, which is makes Big Papa and everyone else on the Dem committee pull their hair out. We're meeting on Zoom and on email vines to figure out what to do about it. I'm new to this party, so I mostly sit back and listen. It's pretty heated. I mean, some people are talking about legal action, others are talking about bum-rushing each picnic with a mob of Dems. From my perspective, none of this sounds very palatable.

Finally, I interrupt to ask the group, "Has anyone talked to Tim?"

Someone asks, who is Tim? I tell them Tim is the grounds guy who is in charge of actually setting up outdoor events for the county, including the picnics – the tents, the catering stations, the transportation, and so on. I've known him for years, since we've collaborated a number of times setting up veteran events. He's a good guy, and I'm pretty sure he doesn't know anything about this silly memo business. Why not ask Tim if he could use some volunteers at the picnics, like before?

"Worth a try," Big Papa says. I ask Ted if he'll email Tim to inquire if I can help out at the picnic – pouring lemonade, setting up tables, whatever. I think it's the same day when Ted reports back. "He said it's fine, you can come to any of the picnics you want."

Crisis averted. Sometimes the simplest solution is the best. And this is one crisis that turns into a real advantage, because Anthony Parisi and I turn the tables on our opponents, starting with the first picnic in May. We are showing up like we own the place, all summer long. We will end up pouring thousands of cups of lemonade and iced tea with a joke or a smile. I'm wearing my VFW hat and chatting with the many older veterans who show up at the picnics.

"Why do you wear that hat?" one of Sue's supporters asks me at a picnic.

"Because I earned it," I reply.

When the DJ at the picnics plays an old-timey number from the 50s, I put down my pitcher and ask some lucky lady to dance. You read that right. Hey, I took five years of swing dance lessons as a younger man, and they are finally coming in handy. I am not exaggerating when I say people are cheering and clapping along with the music each time someone steps out and dances with me; at one picnic, my good friend Heidi and I cut such a rug, we got a standing ovation from the seniors in attendance. I'm not a good dancer, but that's not the point; Anthony and I are clearly having a ball at each picnic, and we almost feel sorry for our opponents because they can only stand on the edge of the tent, arms folded, sulking about the two guys who took over *their* picnics. By the end of the summer, they will try to compensate by having Sue Serino lead a sing-along at the end of each picnic – it's as cringey as it sounds – but the damage has already been done. I'm getting a lot of free advertising just by being my goofy self at these picnics, and it feels good. I'm getting used to trusting myself, and people are noticing. People on both sides.

The High Road

Today is Memorial Day and as usual I'm attending the county ceremony held at the War Memorial in Poughkeepsie. It's always a somber affair, as it should be, as we reflect on the sacrifices of the servicemen and women who have gone before us, especially those who perished while defending our nation. I'm standing in the back row by the parking lot, catching up with my buddy Mickey from the VFW as we wait for the ceremony to start. If you've read *The Low Road*, you know he was a big part of the walk across America. I owe him a lot. Recently he's had some health problems the VA doctors can't seem to figure out, which can bring anyone down. But he seems to be in good spirits today. "So, I got good news and bad news for you," Mickey says, lowering his voice to a whisper. "Good news is I'm voting for you." I already know what the bad news is – Mickey's wife went to high school with Sue Serino and they're still good friends, which means I'm not getting her vote.

"Tell her I'll get over it," I say, wiping away an imaginary tear from my eye.

"No, she's really torn," Mickey says, as his fists flail around. That's a great sign because it means the meds he gets from the VA for his mystery condition are working -- a couple months ago he couldn't bend his fingers. "But I told her, you vote for Sue, and I'll vote for Tom. See? Problem solved." He fake-punches my arm. "Like Meatloaf said, one out of two ain't bad."

"I think it's two out of three," I say.

"Exactly," Mickey says.

A young couple approach me to ask about the "migrant crisis" in Dutchess County, and at first, I assume they are merely more boo-birds trying to get my goat about a powder keg issue – but no, these two genuinely want to find out if there's a way to volunteer and help out the migrant families living at a local motel in Poughkeepsie. (I'm putting "migrant crisis" in quotation marks because it's not really a crisis, although Republicans are sure trying to frame it like that. But come on, 60 nice people moving into the Red Roof Inn while they wait on their asylum paperwork certainly isn't a crisis.) Anyway, I tell the young couple what I know and tell them to contact Yvette Valdés Smith if they want to volunteer, since Yvette has been leading efforts from the start to help these families.

"Good luck with your campaign," the young woman says cheerily before they both drift back into the bustling crowd. "I hope you win." It's refreshing to meet young people who want to do the work to make their community a better place to live; heck, it's refreshing just knowing there are folks under the age of 30 who want to attend Memorial Day ceremonies in America.

Yes, the kids are all right.

An older woman standing on my other side obviously has been listening to the whole conversation, because as soon as the young couple walks away, she lets out a grunt, trying to get my attention. When I pretend not to notice, she only grunts louder. Clearly, she is not going to be ignored. Finally she says, "It's such a shame."

I'm a glutton for punishment I guess, because I turn around with a goofy smile and walk straight into the bear-trap. "What's a shame, ma'am?"

She folds her arms and shoots me a withering gaze that could curdle milk. "Why do you care so much about the illegals when they're the ones kicking veterans out of hotels?"

Here we go. "That's not true," I say. "Veterans were never kicked out of any hotel. That story was made up. And these people are asylum seekers, not illegals."

"Oh my, *asylum* seekers," she says sarcastically. "Give me a break."

I stay on the high road. I tell her how we need more kindness in the world. Then I try to explain how no human being is *illegal*, but it's clear she's having none of it. This is one voter I'll never be able to swing. "I mean, don't you think we need more kindness in the world?"

She ignores my question. "Well, none of this matters," she snarls. "Sue's going to win anyway. I hear she's already got it locked up."

"I hear that, too. But it's only May," I say, mustering a hopeful voice. "Anything can happen. Who knows, maybe you'll change your mind by then."

"What?" she says, recoiling as if bitten by a snake. "I'm not voting for *you*."

"I'm getting that," I say with a broad smile. "Loud and clear." On the outside, I'm smiling because I don't want to give her the satisfaction – but also because it's fun imagining what a joy this woman must be at Thanksgiving when the grandkids visit. But inside I'm wrestling with a profound sadness; I know there are plenty of people in Dutchess County just like this lady who still believe veterans are being kicked out of hotels to make way for "the illegals" even though the story was long ago debunked. The politics of fear is hard at work, once again. Yes, I'm saddened because I realize there are people who will never be able to engage in a reasonable discussion, no matter how nice or accommodating I am. I'm realizing I won't be able to reach everyone with a message of kindness, simply because some folks will never listen. And election or not, I'm learning there are a lot of people in this world who will live their entire lives without experiencing empathy. That's probably the saddest notion of all.

FIFTH CIRCLE

I'VE BEEN eating breakfast once or twice a week at the same diner for the last twenty years. The Eveready in Hyde Park was a local landmark long before TV chef Guy Fieri stopped by on his Food Network show several years back. On any summer weekend between June and September, the place is packed with car show enthusiasts and eco-tourists escaping New York City, chatting away while they take pictures of their food. When the county fair is up and running in August, the line is out the door waiting for tables. As a rule, I only stop by on weekday mornings when it's quiet. I keep to myself and I'm a good tipper, so over the years I've become friends with the owners and some of the waitstaff. And I've been ordering the same thing for so long, they've stopped taking my order. Once, I ordered a salad and threw everyone for a loop. We all have our habits.

I usually sit on the very last stool at the far end of the counter by the orange juice machine, partly because I like my privacy but also to sit as far away as I can from the old men who hold court at the other end of the counter. I think every diner in America has a version of the same three or four retired guys who perch on their stools drinking coffee and talking loudly about what they heard last night on Fox News. Lots of politics, of course. Every sentence seems to start with either, *"Kids these days!"* or *"I remember when!*" – as in, I remember when you could fill up your gas tank, make a telephone call and buy your lunch, all for three bucks. When they really get worked up over something, their wheezy voices fill the whole diner and my buddy Costa has to come out from the back office to shush them. These old timers and I have had an unspoken pact for years now; I leave them alone at their end of the lunch counter, and they do the same for me. They don't know what I do for a living, or what my political views are. They don't even know my name – until today, that is.

"Excuse me," one guy says, tapping me on the shoulder while I'm eating my eggs. He's holding up the latest copy of a local weekly called the *Dutchess News*. The front page features dueling headshots of Sue Serino and yours truly, next to a story that previews all the countywide races this year. "Is this you?"

I point at my picture. "That's me," I say cheerfully. "The other one's Sue Serino."

"Yeah, I know," he says, eyeing me with suspicion like I might be a bank robber, or worse, a socialist. The other members of the court have ambled over to hear the conversation up close; they probably all drew straws to see who gets to poke the bear at the other end of the counter. "You're the Democrat running against Sue?"

"Somebody had to do it," I say, trying to get out of this conversation quickly.

"I don't know about that," another guy says with a sneer. "Everybody loves Sue."

"She's my cousin," a third one adds proudly. "Well, I'm married to her cousin."

What a surprise: more members of the Sue Serino Fan Club here in Hyde Park. I'll bet twenty bucks that one of these dudes is married to the nice lady who tried to kick me out of the farmer's market last month.

"But why would you run against Sue?" the first guy presses,

his voice cracking a bit. "You ask me, it's kind of like – *suicide*." I can hear the anger starting to percolate in their voices, but I'm also getting the impression these guys aren't particularly angry with *me*, personally, for running against Sue – no, they sound like they're more angry with whoever put me up to doing something so crazy.

"Look, I like Sue, too," I say, trying to defuse the situation. "She's great. But don't you think we should always give people a choice? I mean, that's what democracy is all about, right?"

"I guess," the first guy says slowly, like I'm trying to trick him. "I guess."

"He's got you there, Felix," another one says.

"I guess," Felix says again, before turning away. "I just feel sorry for the guy."

They shuffle back to the other end of the counter to continue the discussion, allowing me to finish my breakfast. By the time I pay my check, they're shouting about me in the third person but they've also added Joe Biden, Kamala Harris and Taylor Swift to the list of people who could use a "good talking to." Even when they are agreeing on something, it still sounds like an argument. "I can remember when there weren't *any* Democrats around here at all, not one," Felix says to the others, waving his hands. "Now we got them all over, and every one of them talking about gumdrops and rainbows."

"Yeah, and no clue on how to pay for any of it," another chimes in.

Felix sighs wistfully. "Times sure are changing." They all nod in sadness.

As I make my exit, I figure if they don't like me now, just wait until they actually read that article in the *Dutchess News* where I talk about running my campaign entirely on gumdrops and rainbows – or kindness, to be exact. (All right, get serious for a moment, Tommy boy.) I can make jokes all I want, but I won't have a chance of winning this election without bringing at least some of these folks over to the bright side. There are a lot of voters in Dutchess County who think just like Felix and the boys, older people who are afraid of change and see anyone who even *talks* about change as their sworn enemy. I'll have to work hard to get some of them to drink the Kool-Aid and see the real problems in our community through a lens of kindness instead of the usual cloudy telescope of anger and fear. I know that's a tall order. The good news? If anyone can sell that story, I can. After all, I've been drinking the kindness Kool-Aid for most of my life. Let me explain.

The people closest to me know that my grandmother was a huge part of my life growing up, like a second mom. As a boy, I spent so much time at her house in the country and at the time, I naively thought I was deposited there because she needed my help – tending her beautiful irises and day lilies, measuring the flour and sugar for her entries into the church baking competitions, sharing root beer floats before bedtime – but later I realized she was the one helping me, shielding me from ugly, unsaid things I'd need another book to talk about. The whole time I thought I was saving her, she was saving me. Looking back, I learned so much from my grandmother. For starters, she was the best storyteller I've ever met. As a kid, I only knew her as grandma, a beautiful woman with luxurious silver hair who smoked Kools and made me pancakes for dinner. But by that time, Helen Zurhellen had already lived all over the globe as the wife of a career United States diplomat: Japan, Germany, Israel, Suriname. She was tennis buddies in Tel Aviv with Golda Meier, she sat next to John Wayne at the Vatican for a private audience with the Pope, and in Osaka she hosted heads of state and made Cary Grant laugh at a party. She lived a life most people on this planet only dream about, and she had the stories to back it up. But here's the best part: after such a glamorous life, she took the time to make one little boy feel special, and feel loved, when he needed it the most. I'll admit it wasn't an easy job taking care of me; I was quite a handful, a fat kid with anger issues and a huge chip on his shoulder. But she did it anyway, with silent grace. And over the years, she ingrained in me the one lesson that's changed my life more than anything.

Whenever I got frustrated enough to start kicking the walls – which was often – she would simply say, "Kindness doesn't cost extra." I had no idea what she meant at the time; I figured it was a way of telling me to calm down, count to ten, that sort of thing. She must have said it a lot because much later when I joined the Navy, I would whisper it to myself as a kind of mantra whenever I felt overwhelmed with the job. "Kindness doesn't cost extra." But it took this life of service I'm leading now – the walk across America, running for office, and all the community service in between – to realize exactly what she meant. She wasn't telling me to calm down. She was trying to show me that leading a life of kindness towards others as well as myself is a simple choice. She was teaching me to understand that kindness always open doors, while fear and anger only close them. It's easy to be kind! You just have to *want* to be kind. I've finally learned that lesson over the last several years, and I am not exaggerating when I say it has completely transformed my life. Solving problems is so easy nowadays! All I do is ask myself, what's the solution that brings the most kindness? I just look for the answer that will help the most people. (Which probably makes me the worst politician of all time, I get that!) Inside, I think we all want to be kind, even though we don't follow through sometimes.

Wouldn't it be great if just once – just once! -- we elected a candidate because they are the most kind, instead of being the wealthiest or most charismatic? A candidate who always chooses kindness over fear, no matter how much pressure they are put under. What a revolutionary thought! That's the America I want

The High Road

to live in. And I'm betting on the notion that there are plenty of other folks who feel the same way.

If you read that last paragraph and are now rolling your eyes and thinking, *what a crap-ton of hot nonsense*, trust me, you are not alone. We're almost halfway through the campaign already and I'm getting so many angry calls and messages from Democrat insiders who are wondering what the hell I'm doing. Ted's fielded plenty of the same calls, too. They are all the same: *Why aren't you attacking Sue for taking money from Central Hudson? Why aren't you attacking Sue on her abysmal voting record in the state senate? Why are you wasting your time talking about the homeless and food insecurity? And what the hell is food insecurity, anyway? You need to stick to the issues taxpayers care about. You need to keep hammering the Republicans on wasteful spending and backdoor deals, so people become outraged enough to get off their asses and vote! That's how you win an election. You can't win an election on kindness. Now get out there and attack, attack, attack!*

I think these people are under the impression that being kind automatically means being weak. But it's actually the opposite: kindness *is* strength. That's the secret my grandma taught me when I was growing up. Showing kindness means having the confidence to be vulnerable and let others in. Anger only pushes others away. Now, I'm not under the illusion that I will change these people's minds when it comes to kindness. Old habits die hard, I guess. I'm just trying to get them to understand that I'm never going to change mine.

Today I'm dropping by a fundraiser for my teammate Anthony Parisi at a restaurant in Beacon. He's running for Dutchess County District Attorney, and his wife Sinead (all the countywide candidates call her our "den mom") is doing a fantastic job running his campaign. There's a great turnout at the fundraiser as we all eat pizza and wait for Anthony to say a few words. Assemblymember Jonathan Jacobson is there to introduce him. "I've been doing this a long time," Jonathan says to the crowd. "And I have to say, Anthony is the most coachable candidate I've ever met." And darn it, he's looking right at me when he says it.

Message received, old bean. Loud and clear.

Around the same time, Amelia calls to check in, but I know the real purpose of the call. "People are angry because you're not taking their advice," she says. "Pretty soon they are going to start writing you off."

"I understand," I say. I don't ask specifically what people she is referring to, but I can guess. And I do understand their fury and frustration, I really do. I think they're trying to scare me into being a candidate more like Anthony, but they're really doing the opposite. They don't realize that being kind means more to me than winning an election. It isn't some empty campaign promise I can click off or on when it's convenient. It's who I am. So, when folks like Jonathan or Amelia warn me to get in line or else you're going to find yourself on your own, I have to laugh, because so far, I've pretty much done everything on my own anyway. And it's not like I picked the issues on my platform out of a hat. I chose issues like homelessness and food insecurity because those are the crises in my community I care most about. I wish I could sit all the boo-birds down and teach them the lesson of kindness, the same way my grandma taught me. But I don't have the time, and besides, it's a lesson you have to figure out on your own.

I also wish these boo-birds spent more time out on the campaign trail with me, because they would see the reactions when I start talking to crowds about kindness and compassion, people are listening. They want to find a solution to the homelessness crisis in Dutchess County without stuffing homeless families in the jail. And when they find out thousands of kids right next door are not getting enough to eat, they want to do something about it. I feel the energy every time someone walks up to me at an event and asks, "How can I help?"

Forgive me for believing that kindness can win an election in America.

In Dante's *Inferno*, the Fifth Circle of Hell is reserved for sins of anger, bitterness, and fury. In other words, the haters. (As that other poet Taylor Swift says, *haters gonna hate, hate, hate hate*.) Dante and Virgil cross the foul river Styx to find countless souls drowning in the Stygian marshes – choking on their own rage and blaming the other damned souls around them for their fate. And I don't think it's a coincidence that I'm thinking about my grandma at the same time I'm writing about the anger and mean-spiritedness I'm experiencing on the campaign trail. It makes me wonder what would've happened to me if my grandmother hadn't taught me that lesson of kindness, all those years go. Grandma died in 2007, but she's been with me every day since, whenever I say to myself, *kindness doesn't cost extra*. I wonder what kind of man I would have become without her love and guidance. It makes me realize that thanks to her, I'm built differently than a lot of other folks. We all *want* to be kind. But I think only a few of us strive to do the work to *be* kind, every chance we get. And I have my grandma to thank for that.

I had never heard of food insecurity until March of 2020, when I received a frantic email from the Poughkeepsie City School District (PCSD) asking for help. I was Commander of the Poughkeepsie VFW at the time, and the COVID pandemic had just shut down the world. We were all scrambling to figure out how to care for our kids, our elderly, and our neighbors. Our VFW shut its doors to wait this crisis out, like everyone else. The email from the

PCSD opened my eyes to a crisis happening right in my community. Since all schools were now closed, students at Poughkeepsie schools could not receive their daily school lunch. I was horrified to learn that many of those kids depend on that school lunch as their only square meal of the day; in these tough times, parents are often forced to decide between paying the rent or putting food on the table. And that leaves thousands of children in my city who don't get enough nutritious food to eat. The email from the PCSD was a call for help, asking all local nonprofits if we could supply the thousands of sack lunches necessary to feed these kids over the next few weeks, until the district can figure out a plan to distribute school lunches again. I was shocked and ashamed. How did I not know thousands of young people right in my own community were going hungry for so long? Why has no one shined a light on this problem before? Why did it take a worldwide pandemic to expose the sad fact that millions of kids in America aren't getting enough to eat?

That same day, I started doing research on food insecurity in America. (One thing COVID did give us was a lot of time to waste on the internet.) I was even more shocked and ashamed to learn 1 in 5 kids in America live with hunger – that's 13 million children. Why use a term like "food insecurity" instead of just saying hunger? Because you can't measure hunger. But you can measure households that are food insecure – that is, families that are struggling to put enough food on the table. The United States Department of Agriculture (USDA) reports that approximately 6.4 million households are food insecure – which obviously includes all those kids in my hometown of Poughkeepsie who depend on their school lunch every week. Perhaps the most shocking revelation for me was learning about how food insecurity can be devastating to a child's mental and physical health, not to mention their performance in school. It can increase the risk of everything from asthma to anxiety for a growing child. I sat there in front of my laptop, motionless; there are many kinds of sadness in the world, but for me, there are none more profound than learning kids in my own neighborhood will never enjoy the childhood I had, generations ago.

Also that same day, I get a call from my dear friend Christa Hines at Hudson River Housing. She received the same email, and it's clear I'm not the only one shocked and ashamed. "What are we going to do about this?" she asks me. So together we come up with a plan to muster some volunteers and set up a sack lunch assembly line at the empty VFW to pump out as many nutritious meals as possible. Christa will take care of finding some hardy souls to join us, and I will acquire as much peanut butter, jelly, bread, sliced cheese, juice boxes, apples, snacks and brown bags as I can find. When local grocery stores find out what we're doing with all this stuff, they donate a lot of it. And for a few weeks, it was simply beautiful to see people in masks and food service gloves working as a team to churn out 100 or 200 lunches a day. I lost count of how many total bags we sent over to the school district, but it had to be in the thousands.

Christa and I certainly didn't solve food insecurity in Poughkeepsie during those several weeks, but we moved the needle. We worked together and made an impact. We experienced the power of kindness. People often ask me, how do you find the energy to do so much service? And I always answer, you've got it all wrong; when you lead a life of service, the energy finds you. Whenever I am blessed with an opportunity to make a stranger's life better, it's a unique rush I wouldn't trade for anything in the world.

And I certainly wouldn't trade it for $250,000 in corporate donations.

Some of these issues I'm talking about in my stump speeches, like homelessness, food insecurity and veteran outreach, are obviously passions I've brought with me from past experiences. But

I'm getting equally fired up on causes I'm learning about for the first time on the campaign trail, too. One of these causes is the mighty struggle of our labor unions, which I will describe in more detail later in the book. Another is the importance of defending disability rights in our communities, which I'm going to talk about now since it's June when I am invited by Lisa Tarricone to attend the TRI Inclusion Festival held on the grounds of the FDR Library and Museum in Hyde Park. And just like that email from the PCSD exposed me to food insecurity, this experience will open my eyes wide as I learn about the efforts of disability advocates to make public spaces in America accessible to all.

A few weeks before the festival, Lisa invites me to the offices of her advocacy organization Taconic Resources International (TRI) in Poughkeepsie. (It's actually a short walk from my apartment; I must have passed it a thousand times without knowing.) She's done the same for my opponent, of course, since TRI is a nonprofit and has to be impartial. But Lisa doesn't care who wins the election. She wants the next County Executive to understand how frustrating it is trying to convince municipalities in Dutchess to make vital changes to everything from schools to sidewalks so those with disabilities can enjoy the same access as everyone else. The Americans with Disabilities Act or ADA is a civil rights law passed back in 1990 to ensure cities and towns make the necessary upgrades to public spaces, but 33 years later, most municipalities and businesses have ignored the law. That's certainly true in Dutchess County; only one small village out of the thirty municipalities (two cities, twenty towns, and eight villages) in our county have even responded to TRI's request to do more. That village is Tivoli, where mayor Joel Griffith has quietly improved the sidewalks and upgraded the local park to include things like ramps and grab bars in the restrooms.

Around the same time, I attend a panel discussion in Poughkeepsie about the housing crisis. I'm the only candidate there, so I'm sure it's one of those events that don't matter Jonathan was talking about, but here I am anyway sitting in the back row listening to reps from different state agencies share the stories of people they work with who are denied housing by landlords who routinely break the law. I'm gaining a lot of insight from the conversation, but the one thing that stands out for me is something the guy from the NY Division of Human Rights says towards the end: the most common violation – by far – when it comes to being denied housing is disability. Landlords don't want to accommodate anyone with disabilities because it will cost them money to make those upgrades. That's disgraceful. That means the people who need help the most when it comes to finding a safe, secure place to live are also the ones denied housing the most. I wonder where dirty landlords land in Dante's nine rings of Hell. Hopefully, rock bottom.

When the TRI Inclusion Festival comes around in late June, I'm honestly excited to be a part of it. I show up early, and I stay until the end. I meet so many disability advocates who are working hard in their communities to bring change, and I listen to their stories. Mayor Joel from Tivoli is one of the keynote speakers and we strike up a friendship on the spot. A month ago, I had no idea this vibrant subculture even existed, and today, I make my first campaign promise to Lisa: if I get elected, one of the first things I do will be appointing a Chief Disability Officer whose primary job will be to encourage towns in our county to follow the ADA and make the necessary upgrades, using either the carrot or stick. After all, it's not just the law, it's the right thing to do.

I'm there for the whole four hours, soaking in the stories and finding out all I can about the work of these heroes. Sadly, my opponent shows up for the last 15 minutes of the festival with her entourage, as most people are leaving. For her, it's just another photo-op, I guess. For me, it's an opportunity to get that rush that only comes with serving others. I'm hoping someone sees the difference, but I'm good if they don't.

Fifth Circle

As I'm walking out to my truck, one of the festival volunteers who checked me in stops me on the sidewalk. "I just want to say, thank you for staying the whole time," she says, nodding her head. "You've got my vote."

Hey, somebody noticed the difference! I only need about 35,000 other people to notice between now and November and I have this election all sewn up. Easy peasy.

I'm at the Eveready again, minding my own business when I get another tap on my shoulder. "Is this you?" It's Felix again, but this time when I turn around – to my utter surprise – he's holding up a copy of my book *The Low Road*. I'd forgotten I had given copies to a couple of the waitstaff at the diner who were interested in the walk across America. Felix is pointing to my picture on the back cover, the one where I'm in Nebraska about to get pummeled by a thunderstorm. Wow, I sure looked thinner back then. Also, I looked a lot happier.

"That's me, all right," I say. "How did you get that book?"

Felix has a sheepdog look on his face. "Well, we've been talking about you a lot, behind your back. You know, when you're not here."

"Good things?"

"No," he says. "But the girls behind the counter, they stood up for you. They said you walked across the country to help veterans. Is that true?"

I nod my head. "That is true. I'm a Navy veteran myself." And just like that, I'm surrounded on my stool by these retired guys who are peppering me with questions about the walk. Where did you sleep? What did you eat? How many pairs of shoes did you go through? I tell them the mountain lion story in Oregon, and the Nutter Butters story in Wyoming. My breakfast has long gone cold, but I don't mind because these guys are hanging on every word as I give them the highlights of my journey. Then I tell them the story about my walking stick getting stolen outside the Dunkin' Donuts in Ithaca, New York.

"Fucking Ithaca," one guy says. "I knew it." They all nod.

A week or so later, I'm back at the diner when something happens which busts the flood gates wide open and turns our relationship into an all-out bro-mance. I'm back at my usual place at the end of the counter eating my eggs when I hear a big commotion behind me. I swivel around to see one of the old men on the floor, flat on his back. He must have lost his balance getting up from his stool and hit the tile floor, hard. Felix and a couple of the other guys are trying to help him up, but he's too much weight for them. So, I swoop in and scoop him off the floor, slipping my arms under his armpits until he can put his feet back on the ground. It all happens in a few seconds. The guy is all right; there's no real damage other than his embarrassment for causing a scene. His backside will feel sore in the morning, that's for sure. I don't think much of it – I'm a big guy, and I pick up things heavier than this gentleman all the time – but the old men at the other end of the counter are looking at me like I just parted the Red Sea.

Afterwards, every time I walk in the place one of them will say, "There's our hero!" and they'll grab anyone who happens to walk by to ask them if they know the story about how Tommy saved a man's life *right there*, pointing to the floor like there should be a historical marker on the exact spot. Give it another month, and I'm guessing the story will have morphed into the time Tommy picked him up with one arm and performed CPR with the other at the same time. I'm flattered, of course. But I can't help but notice how in the span of a few weeks, the walls between me and Felix's crew have come tumbling down. Their initial reactions of anger and blunt suspicion have dissolved into honest curiosity and affection. How did that happen? What did I do to break down those walls, other than scooping a guy up from the floor? For the rest of the campaign, these guys will be some of my biggest supporters, always asking me how it's going out there on the trail. They secretly pay for my breakfast some days, and I do the same for them. Our conversations are a whole lot different than when we first met a month ago.

"You're going to do all right in this election, big fella," one guy will say.

"I would vote for you if Sue wasn't my cousin," another will say.

I'll take it. I'm not especially religious, but I'm grateful for whatever force in the universe that turned these gentlemen 180 degrees from enemies to friends in such a short time. I'd like to think that force is kindness. And I understand I probably don't have enough time left in this election cycle to spread the gospel of kindness to all the other angry souls who live in Dutchess County. But that's sure not going to stop me from trying. I know I'm not alone, even though it feels that way sometimes. In his excellent book *Across That Bridge*, civil rights icon John Lewis wrote, "I find myself asking, 'Why do we have to be so mean?' Is there something in the air we breathe or the water we drink that incites us to bring one another down, to violate one another with so much glee?" And closer to home, I have teammates like Yvette Valdés Smith, Jim Rogers and Kenya Gadsden who are talking about compassion and empathy, too. Kenya's vision for the county clerk's office is a welcoming place where people can come for more than merely their fishing license. Jim is talking about transforming Family Court into a place that truly cares about the welfare of children. And Yvette is championing the cause of migrant workers who have been met with nothing but anger and hate in Dutchess County. We are all working towards the same goal that John Lewis taught us years ago. We're opening doors with kindness, instead of closing them with fear.

SIXTH CIRCLE

My first door knock is on a quiet country lane called Skunks Misery Road. With a name like that, I figure anybody who lives there must have a sense of humor, which can be a real benefit when a large, sweaty ogre carrying campaign literature suddenly appears on the front stoop. The twisty road is located up in the northeast corner of the county near the town of Millerton – farm country, where there are generally more cows than people. But I'm not out here today in God's green acre because of the scenery. No, I'm here because according to the campaign research on my MiniVAN app, Democrats have never knocked on these doors before. As in, ever.

It's a warm, sunny Saturday in the dog days of summer as I make the drive up to northern Dutchess. An hour ago, I was down in Poughkeepsie at Democrat HQ with all the other candidates to cut our turfs for the day, before we disperse to neighborhoods all over Dutchess County. A young guy named Logan with flowing blonde locks and a laptop is the official keeper of the turfs – that is, he's the one who controls the master list of addresses and voting records for every Democrat in the county with the MiniVAN manager software. All the candidates have the MiniVAN app on their phones, so it's easy for Logan to send each of us a territory of twenty or thirty homes in the same area so we can make a day out of knocking on doors, engaging with fellow Democrats, handing out palm cards to anyone who will accept them, and reminding folks to make a plan to vote in November. Some people like to canvas in groups, others prefer to go alone. My teammate Anthony Parisi and his wife Sinead are the Olympic gold medalists for this activity, hands down; I might attend more events than anyone else, but I wouldn't be surprised if they are knocking on more doors than Kenya, Jim and me combined. Speaking of Kenya: we're trying to keep this an in-house secret, but she is out-of-commission for a month or two this summer after undergoing a very necessary hip replacement surgery. The rest of us are trying our best to pick up the slack, handing out her palm cards and speaking on her behalf at the meet-and-greets and house parties while she recuperates. There's no replacing Kenya's energy or talent for public speaking on the campaign trail, though. We can't wait until she's back.

In an off-year election where turnout is usually low, knocking on doors is probably the best way to get out the vote. It doesn't cost any money, so it's a good alternative when you don't have the funds for bulk mailers, billboards or TV spots. It does cost the candidate a lot in time and energy, however. Some door knocks can be discouraging, and in some cases, downright dangerous: the dog might be loose, the porch steps might be slippery, or the nice Democrat family who used to live there have been replaced by a guy with *Let's Go Brandon* flags flying all over. (The MiniVAN app makes mistakes, for sure.) Some people won't open the door because they automatically put you in the same category as a traveling salesperson or Jehovah's Witness. But on the bright side, there are plenty of decent people out there who don't mind opening the door to speak with a candidate who shares their views and passions – especially if they've never had a candidate knock on their door before. Which is why I'm out here alone today, tracking down my very first lead on Skunks Misery Road.

I find the right house number on a battered mailbox and pull over to the other side of the road. The MiniVAN app tells me a couple lives here, both registered Democrats; this should be a great place to start my day. But when I get out of the truck, I notice the loose gravel driveway twisting straight up to the house on top of a tall hill. It must be a quarter mile. I doubt my truck could make it up there; considering the shape I'm in, I doubt I can make it on foot, either. But I didn't come this far for nothing. So, I begin my slow ascent up the gravel driveway, my arms straight out for balance. I want to say a little prayer, but I'm not sure who the patron saint is for fat guys trying to avoid a heart attack while climbing a mountain. Every few steps, I stop to catch my breath. Finally, I get to the top and lean on the porch railing, wheezing like an old accordion. I'm about to reach for the doorbell when I realize the guy has been standing behind the screen door the whole time, watching my death climb on his driveway.

"You've already got my vote," he says before I can get a word out. "Anyone crazy enough to walk up that driveway in the summertime has earned it."

Turns out he's read an interview with me in the *Millerton News*, so he already knows who I am. More good news: we're both Navy veterans, so we instantly have a lot to talk about, even though we're from different generations. "I would let you in," he says from behind the screen. "But my wife's got the COVID." We stand there for ten minutes, mostly swapping Navy stories but also talking about the election. We talk about how difficult it is to get emergency services to come up here to northern Dutchess. "I like what you're saying about the homeless folks, and food for the kids," he says before we part ways. "It's a damn shame what they're doing. Keep up the good work. I hope you win."

The walk back down to my truck is a lot easier than the walk up, thanks in part to gravity but also because I'm feeling so energized by our conversation. It's evidence that my message of kindness and inclusion is getting around, even in rural parts of the county where candidates never seem to visit. I will knock on approximately fifteen more doors today – some interactions are positive, some not. But every time I talk to someone, I feel like it's time well spent. When I'm knocking on doors, I'm reminded that many people have no idea who the candidates are, much less what they stand for. When I get a chance to talk about the homelessness crisis in Dutchess County, for example, a lot of folks are surprised. They really don't know what's at stake in this election, and that's probably why voter turnout is so low. Out here, I'm learning people *do* care, but only if they know there's something to care about. And it's my job to convince them there's a hell of a lot to care about in this election.

Call time has gone from bad to worse. When I started back in April, I enjoyed a good streak of beginner's luck, but that has long dried up. Now it's July and I mostly end up leaving phone messages. It's rare when someone does pick up, and usually they hang up after a few seconds. It's demoralizing, for sure. I've been told time and again that call time is a necessary evil, since it's the quickest way to get big dollar donors on my side. Frankly, I'm not seeing that. I think the call lists I've been given have been picked over – about a quarter of the phone numbers are disconnected, or just plain incorrect. When I do get someone on the line, they tell me they've already given to Democrats like Congressman Pat Ryan and State Senator Michelle Hinchey – who aren't even running this year. The well has run dry. But getting turned down by a potential donor isn't the worst part of call time. I've even gotten used to the angry hang-ups; I don't take them personally anymore. No, the worst calls are the ones where the person is *waiting* for you to call. Yes, there are people out there sitting at home (or in their hidden bunker, I imagine, surrounded by barbed wire) who want candidates to call, so they can unload their conspiracy theories and political diatribes on a captive audience. They have no intention of making a donation, but they know the candidate will probably stay on the line, in hopes of getting one. To illustrate, allow me to share a brief snippet of my thirty minutes in call time Hell with a guy named Pete.

"Is this Peter?"

There's a long pause. I can hear TV news blaring in the background. "Yes."

"Hi, Peter. This is Tommy Zurhellen, and I'm the Democrat running for Dutchess County Executive this year. How are you today?"

"Fine," he says. "I'm not a Democrat. I haven't voted in a long time." This is normally the moment I expect people to hang up, but he's still on the line. I can hear him munching loudly on something, maybe potato chips.

"So, you're an independent? Great! We need everyone this year because –"

"I'm not giving you any money unless you can promise me zero taxes."

"Say again?"

"You heard me," he says, his voice heating up. "I'm not giving you a donation unless you promise me zero taxes."

I'm waiting for the punchline, but none comes. "I can't promise you that. No one can."

"Exactly! See? You see?" I'm not sure if he's still talking to me, the talking heads blaring on his TV, or just himself. But this leads to an extended rant about how we're all screwed because of taxes. I'll say this for Pete, he knows his stuff. Income tax, property tax, sales tax, capital gains tax. "They get you coming and going, do you see?" I'm guessing he was a CPA or tax attorney in his former life. Now I'm imagining him pacing back and forth inside a remote cabin with no windows and newspaper clippings covering the walls. I feel sorry for the guy, so I don't hang up. I'm also learning a lot about the New York tax code. This call's going to take a while, so I prop my feet up on my desk and reach into the minifridge for some leftover kung pao chicken. Occasionally I throw something into the conversation, just so he knows I'm still here. When the rant is finally over, Pete sounds exhausted. I think I might be the only one with the patience to get this far into his tirade, because he surprises me by saying, "Look, I can't remember the last time I voted, but I'm going to vote this year." He doesn't say if he's voting for me, but hey, I'll take it.

"That's great," I say. "Would you like to donate to my campaign?"

"Send me an email." He hangs up, leaving me exhausted.

It's only July, and I feel like I'm running out of gas. And it's not just the drudgery of call time that is draining my spirit. I haven't had one day off since the county convention back in February. Compared to my countywide teammates, I'm at a disadvantage because I'm the only one doing this dance alone. They all have wonderful families who are supporting them at every turn; I have a studio apartment with an empty fridge waiting for me at the end of the day. Am I jealous? You bet. But that's not the problem. I'm burning the candle at both ends without any regard for my health; if I was thirty years old, I would just tell myself to suck it up and keep moving. But I am not thirty, and as I mentioned at the start of this book I am in the worst shape of my life. For someone like me, getting no sleep and only eating pigs in blankets between events is a recipe for disaster.

It's getting to the point where my teammates are noticing. When we show up together for events, I'll immediately find a chair in the corner rather than float around shaking hands and making introductions like I should be doing. I just can't physically stand up for very long. "You don't look so good," Jim will whisper candidly. And Sinead has silently taken on the duties of tying my shoes (which are always untied) like I'm one of her kids.

This is getting to be embarrassing. I'm worn out with four months left to go. If I'm going to go the distance, I need to find an oasis. It's a little late to take up new hobbies, though, and I don't have the free time to hunker down with a good book for hours on end, like I used to. With four months left in this downward spiral through the underworld, I desperately need to add something to my life that has absolutely nothing to do with campaigning or call time. Something positive. Somewhere I can be invisible. Something to help me breathe again.

I read a lot of books. Like, a lot. Some people get addicted to sugar at an early age, or knitting, or telenovelas, or playing the cello – but for me, holding a book in my hands and feeling the pages slip through my fingertips is the one joy in life I can't do without. A mug of black coffee in the morning is a distant second. And it doesn't even matter if it's a good book or not. My habit started with a tattered stash of old *Classics Comics* I found in grandma's attic, and by the time I graduated to *Treasure Island* and *The Lord of the Rings* in middle school, my world was changed forever. Luckily, it's not a very expensive habit as long as I keep my library fines in check. I will admit I'm not one of those people who can read books off a screen. I've certainly tried it; audiobooks, too. I need the satisfying sound of flipping pages in my life! And I'm not prepared to debate Bill Nye on this, but I truly believe there is a static electricity generated by fingers rasping against the pages of a book, which fuels the imagination.

My writing students at Marist start to tune out whenever I get to the "static electricity/imagination" theory part of the course. Well, most of them do.

Sixth Circle

I'll read just about anything, too, from Norwegian crime thrillers to survival guides for the impending zombie apocalypse. Thankfully, I am still finding time to read despite the never-ending, merry-go-round schedule of the campaign trail; but as you might expect, my reading queue these days is full of political memoirs. I'm trying to glean some insight and inspiration from the stories of people running for office for the first time. There are certainly more than enough political memoirs to choose from; it seems every public servant in America seeking a job in Washington D.C. is obliged to publish their story as a rite of passage, whether they've written the book or not. Some are excellent, and some are not. But out of all these "origin story" memoirs the one I admire most, and find the most inspirational, is *I Swear* by Katie Porter. As far as I'm concerned, it's the only book to read (and re-read) if you're like me, trying to navigate the scary and surprising world of politics for the first time.

I already knew Katie Porter as the tough U.S. Representative from California who skewers CEOs and cabinet officials in Congressional hearings, using smart questions and her trademark whiteboard. But until I read her 2023 memoir *I Swear: Politics is Messier Than My Minivan* about her own journey into politics, I had no idea how much she had to struggle just to be able to sit in that chair. I'm not going to pretend our paths are similar – for starters, she's a single mom of three, and I'll never know that level of exhaustion – but our stories do have some things in common. We're both college professors, for one, and we both have experienced lifetimes of weight and body-image issues. Most importantly, we both seem to be doing this for the same reasons; in the book, when someone asks why she's running for office, she responds, "I just want to fix some shit."

Amen, sister.

The book just came out this April, but I've already ruined my dog-eared copy with layers of coffee and fast-food stains because I keep it in my truck. That way, I'll always have something inspirational to read as I sit waiting for the next event to start. (Another campaign tip: never be the first to arrive at an event – especially your own. And no matter how many people show up, talk up the "amazing turnout" on social media.) The most sobering part of Katie Porter's story for me is when she finally gets to Congress, tired and stressed but at the same time, hungry to "fix some shit." She talks to another first-time colleague and wonders how he has so much energy doing this job? His reply is blunt. He says her only job as a member of Congress is to simply show up and be Vote 218, which is the number of votes needed to pass a bill in the House. That's it.

I love what Katie writes about that moment: "My colleague's message was clear: I was doing it wrong. I had only myself to blame for being worn out and frustrated. My hard work in asking questions and trying to change policy was visible to my colleagues; they just thought it was a waste of time."

You're doing it wrong. Boy, I can sure identify with that.

Luckily for America, Katie Porter didn't listen to the boo-birds and kept doing things her way, continuing her fight to expose corporate greed and corruption because she knows it's the right thing to do. And lucky for me, I look at the choice she made to follow her own path and feel confident that I'm running for all the right reasons, too – even when people around me are constantly shouting, you're doing it wrong. Running for Congress is a lot different than running for Dutchess County Executive, of course, but I think the stakes for the person running are exactly the same, no matter the office. Namely, are you going to be able to look at yourself in the mirror when the campaign is over, whether you win or lose? Are you going to be able to look your friends in the eye?

Are you going to be able to keep your soul?

As I mentioned before, there's no shortage of politicians who try their hand at writing a book. But it seems there are very few writers and creatives in America who try their hand at politics. I've only found a few scattered examples: Upton Sinclair running for Governor in California in 1934, Gore Vidal running for Congress in 1960, and Norman Mailer running for mayor of New York City in 1969. (They all lost.) This is my fifth book, so I guess I'm in this "exclusive" club, too. But my favorite story of a writer who decided to plunge deep into politics is about Hunter S. Thompson, who famously ran for sheriff in his hometown of Aspen, Colorado in 1970. Thompson is the author of *Fear Loathing in Las Vegas* and is widely regarded as the father of Gonzo journalism. At first, his campaign for sheriff was merely a satiric joke, an entertaining bit of dramatic theatre made to piss off the establishment in Aspen, and beyond; this was 1970, after all. When he started, Thompson didn't think he had a chance to actually win; he officially named his political party FREAK POWER, and its campaign symbol was a red fist with two thumbs. His six-point plan for Aspen included replacing the city streets with grass, installing stocks in front of the courthouse to punish dishonest dope dealers, and changing the name of Aspen to "Fat City." He even shaved his head so he could call the Republican also running for sheriff his "long-haired opponent."

It wasn't all fun and games, however. He received numerous death threats, including one sent to city hall threatening to use dynamite if Thompson was elected. But I think the thing that wore on him the most as the election loomed closer – even more than the death threats – was the realization that he could actually *win*. When he declared his candidacy, he could do and say anything he wanted, simply because he had nothing to lose. This was all supposed to be a joke he could write about later. But now, it wasn't a joke anymore; a lot of people in Aspen identified with the spirit of his wackadoodle ideas, even if they didn't take the ideas seriously. What would Thompson do if he won? He hadn't thought that far. As election day got closer, his demeanor soured because he felt the pressure.

I've been thinking about that story of Hunter S. Thompson a lot lately, because I can identify with the arc of his wild tale. My campaign has never been a joke to me, of course – but five months ago, I was a candidate with nothing to lose. I wasn't given much of a chance of winning by anybody, except maybe my mom. (Thanks, Mom.) I was a last-minute replacement for Robin Lois, my cousin was (and is) my campaign manager, and my opponent was too well-liked and too well-funded. Most folks scoffed when I created a platform entirely based on kindness. I didn't have any political contacts or bigtime donors in my corner, but at the same time, I didn't have any pressure to win weighing me down, either. Now that we have passed the halfway mark to election day, I can definitely say I'm feeling the pressure build, more and more each day. I can feel the anxiety rising in my throat and chest. Why? Because now there are thousands of people who truly believe in me, and I don't want to let them down. And because for the first time, just like Thompson, I am realizing I have a chance to win this thing.

Listen, I didn't agree to this journey on a lark. I didn't become a candidate to better my career or pad my resume, either. I'm here because I want to help people. I'm here because like Katie Porter, I just want to fix some shit. With kindness, of course.

Physically I feel like I'm at the end of my rope, so I push myself to find an oasis – a way to retreat from the constant grind of the campaign trail, if only for a moment. And I'm proud to report I've found *two* oases: first, I talk to my friend Renee at Dutchess Outreach and ask if I could volunteer a couple hours a week stocking shelves at the food pantry in Poughkeepsie. Second, I get my ass to the gym. Thursday and Saturday mornings, I'm hiding in the back row of an aerobics class at Mike Arteaga's gym in Poughkeepsie. The official name of the class is Group Blast. I try to keep up as best

Sixth Circle

I can, but there are certain moves in the 40-minute class that a guy my size should never attempt, for safety's sake. Not so much my safety, but the safety and wellbeing of the others around me; if I go down, I'm probably taking a half dozen or so retired ladies with me. The instructor is a wonderfully patient woman named Michelle who probably feels sorry for the slow-moving 400lbs. guy in the back trying to be invisible.

You might be saying, how is stocking shelves at a pantry or doing the macarena at the gym any different than the physical exertion you're already putting out? You may think, work is work. But that's not the case. For me, volunteering at the food pantry is an easy escape, because I don't have to engage anyone while I'm arranging the canned goods or restocking the toilet paper. I love knowing the work I'm doing will benefit others, in a small and anonymous way. Putting in my time at the gym twice a week with Michelle's blast class does the same thing – I get there, sweat for 40 minutes in the back row without engaging anyone, and then get out. No one who works at the Dutchess Outreach pantry knows who I am (except my friend Renee, of course.) They just think I'm the sleepy guy who comes in for two hours every Monday morning to stock the shelves. And no one in the blast class knows who I am, either.

Well, at least not yet.

This minor detour on health might sound trivial to some. Indeed, I can hear my younger self saying, *stop whining and start working.* But I'm not my younger self anymore, and I'm not the guy who walked across America four years ago. For the first time, I'm realizing that's a good thing. I'm learning so much on this journey, but perhaps my biggest takeaway will be listening to my body and respecting its limitations, which is something I have never done before. Win or lose, I don't want to limp across the finish line when this election is finally over. And I don't want other people having to tie my own shoes (although I'm eternally grateful to Sinead for her quiet kindness.) So, here's another campaign tip for anyone considering a run for office: install time in your schedule for little things that have absolutely nothing to do with your campaign. Nine months is a very long time to spend day and night doing only one thing. Find your own detours. I think it's easier if you have a family, because you can lean on the people who love you unconditionally. But you're going it alone, like me, you still have to seek out your own *oubliettes*, that is, the secret rabbit holes where you can detach and recharge your batteries. I'm not exaggerating when I say something so small could save your life, because I'm pretty sure it helped save mine.

I mentioned my friend Renee a few moments ago. She is the CEO at Dutchess Outreach, which operates both the food pantry and the Lunch Box community kitchen at their facility on Hamilton Street in Poughkeepsie. Like Christa Hines at HRH and my new friend Yvette Valdés Smith, she is a true partner-in-kindness I know I can rely on; we've coordinated together on several projects over the years. Anyway, she wants to sit down separately with both candidates for Dutchess County Executive to talk about – you guessed it – food insecurity, particularly with young people. Whoever wins the election, she wants the next County Executive to know what's at stake for so many families dealing with hunger on a daily basis, and more importantly, she is hoping they will act to do something about it.

We agree to meet at the Starbucks across from Marist. For me, school is still out until the end of August, so the place is relatively empty now; when students return, it becomes a situation I try to avoid. Renee is already here when I arrive, with various info sheets, flowcharts and diagrams spread out over a table. She looks eager to dig into a crash course on food insecurity. "I don't want to hurt your feelings, my friend," I say, sitting down across from her. "But this is one subject I don't think I need a primer for."

"I figured that," she says, smiling. "But I have to treat you and Sue exactly the same." I know she's right. New York Attorney General Tish James recently sent out a memo to all nonprofit organizations in the state, reminding them of their responsibilities in staying neutral when it comes to supporting one candidate over another in elections. Marist has certainly read the memo; and as we will see later in this book, other nonprofits will completely ignore it.

I tell Renee my story about the sack lunch project Christa and I created at the VFW to help fight food insecurity for Poughkeepsie kids during COVID. It's obvious we are on the same page when it comes to finding solutions for food insecurity in our community. Renee knows I'm the only candidate in Dutchess County even talking about hunger, but she can't acknowledge it. Officially, anyway. She also knows I'm not doing my campaign any favors by sticking with the issues I'm truly passionate about, like food insecurity and the homelessness crisis.

"I should have stuck with taxes and affordable housing," I say, and we both laugh. "My life would be a lot easier." Then I ask her a question that makes her eyes light up. "Renee, what's on your wish list of things the county could help with?"

She rattles off a few initiatives, and they all sound great. But the one that immediately catches my ear is one that I've been seriously thinking about, too: creating a community restaurant in Poughkeepsie large enough to really make a difference for the thousands of people here dealing with hunger. You may have heard of Jon Bon Jovi's version of a community restaurant called the Soul Kitchen in New Jersey. It's a place where no one is denied a nutritious meal because they can't afford it. I would love to see a place like that thrive in my hometown of Poughkeepsie, because it's so sorely needed.

Before we part, I let Renee in on a secret I won't be announcing until next month; I figure she and her entire team at Dutchess Outreach would be the happiest to hear it. I tell her if I win, I'm donating my entire salary as County Executive – all four years – to fighting food insecurity with our young people in Dutchess. The salary is currently $147,000 per year, so that means more than a half-million dollars will go directly to programs that make sure our kids never go hungry again. That's a lot of money going to where it's needed most. It won't solve the whole problem, but I figure it's a wonderful start.

"That's amazing," Renee says.

I shrug my shoulders. "If I win, you'll be my first call."

I've had this idea of donating my salary for a while now, ever since my birthday in April. Big Papa wasn't a huge fan, not because it's not noble but because it might come off as a campaign gimmick. But I think people realize by now that I'm not doing this for the gimmicks. I figure there are kids living right down the street who could use that money a hell of a lot more than I ever could. When I announce it in August, and encourage my opponent to make the same pledge, the question I get the most will be, "How are you going to pay rent, or even eat?" Not to worry, because Sinead and Yvette have promised I can come over for dinner anytime I want. (Sinead recommends Pizza Fridays.) Seriously, though, I'm not doing this for votes – if I was, I'd probably make the announcement in October, closer to the election. I'm doing it for the same exact reason I started this journey in the first place: because I believe when you are given a chance to help others, you must take it.

Later, Renee will tell me an elected official we both know well approached her to ask, "Why is Tommy saying there are hungry children in Dutchess County?" She wouldn't tell me what she said in response, but I can imagine it included a lot of flowcharts, diagrams and info sheets spread across the table.

It's the last Saturday in July and I'm out knocking on doors again in the rural part of the county, only a few miles from Skunks Misery Road – and you know what, I feel like I've got a new spring in my step. Maybe it's my imagination, but those blast classes at the gym have given my legs, and confidence, a bit of a boost. When I cut my turf for the day with Logan back at Democrat HQ, he tells me I should be concentrating on more urban neighborhoods like Poughkeepsie, where it's easy to go from house to house, but I plan on saving my hometown for last. I'm still trying to engage the families up here in the woods who have never been canvassed before, many of which are new to Dutchess County. Case in point: today I meet a thirty-something dad who moved up from Brooklyn with his family two years ago. He might be older, since I notice he's wearing a Hüsker Dü t-shirt; maybe he just has good taste in music. He's outside his garage tinkering with a half-assembled ATV. The front yard is littered with toys; I notice there's no traffic on this road and the next house must be a half mile down, which makes this a prime spot for kids to play – not exactly something you find in Brooklyn. He tells me they have two little ones, a boy and a girl. Then I get into my standard sixty-second County Executive elevator pitch, but he stops me when I say I'm endorsed by Planned Parenthood. "I don't need to hear any more," he says, smiling. "You've got our votes." Then he scratches his head. "What does a County Executive do?"

"It's kind of like your Borough President, down in Brooklyn. Just with a lot less money." I look up and down the empty road. "You get many politicians coming out here?"

"Honestly? You're the first."

I believe it, brother.

SEVENTH CIRCLE

I'M WALKING the picket line outside an assisted living facility called the Pines alongside members of the United Healthcare Workers union, and I'm having the time of my life. When I agreed to run for Dutchess County Executive back in February, this was exactly the daydream I had pictured: getting out into the community and finding some of that good, necessary trouble every day. This is merely an informational picket and not a strike, but I couldn't tell you the difference because the energy today is off the charts. There's fifty or so union members here walking together in a big loop, wearing their 1199 SEIU colors and toting signs with messages like QUALITY CARE OVER PROFIT and I KNOW I'M WORTH MORE THAN 1.25%. Yvette Valdés Smith is here, too, along with her two young boys in tow. The boys look bored on arrival, but they soon realize they are passing out whistles, and in no time this picket line sounds more like a Mardi Gras parade, with cheers, endless chants of "Union Busting is Disgusting!" and yes, plenty of whistle bursts from Yvette's kids, whose faces are slowly turning blue with the effort. The youngest is only four and he's having a hard time keeping up on foot, so I let him hitch a ride on my shoulders – which means I get a good half-hour of staccato whistling directly into my left ear. Luckily, I went to a lot of heavy metal shows as a kid, so I figure the damage to my auditory nerve has already been done.

As we march, I'm listening to the personal stories of these healthcare heroes as they simply ask for fair wages and fair working conditions. One woman tells me that often there aren't enough healthcare aides to cover each floor at the Pines, which can be potentially dangerous for the patients living there. She says they are stretched too thin to properly serve the clients. Another woman tells me the union has tried to bring the corporation to the table to negotiate a new contract, but the corporation has been dragging its feet. During COVID these people were classified as essential workers, and now, they feel forgotten. With inflation and the cost of living these days, they are telling me it's impossible to make ends meet anymore. And that's why we're out here today, trying to raise awareness that these folks are being treated unfairly.

I know the Pines well, because a lot of elderly veterans have been housed here, including my favorite veteran of all time, Stu Vidal. Stu was a World War II veteran and a member of my VFW Post in Poughkeepsie. He was the first person I talked to when I joined the Post, and he told me the story of working on an airfield on the island of Tinian in the South Pacific in 1945, watching the Enola Gay take off with the atom bomb, bound for Hiroshima. He was a mentor for me and many others; when he died at the age of 103, countless people came forward to tell their own Stu Vidal story – how kind he was, and how he saved the lives or fortunes of people all over Poughkeepsie with his quiet compassion. He's the kindest person I've ever met, and he's still my role model. I visited him at the Pines towards the end of his amazing life, and all he wanted to talk about was my walk across America, which I had completed six months before. Well, that and baseball. That was the kind of guy Stu was, and I miss him every day.

When I visited Stu Vidal at the Pines, I was happy to see how well the staff there were taking care of him. I've visited veterans at other facilities in the area, and I would feel so sad – and more than a bit angry – when I saw first-hand the neglect and apathy of the people charged with the welfare of these American heroes. I didn't see that at the Pines, with Stu or the other vets I've visited there over the years. Honestly, it felt like family there, and I was relieved that Stu was receiving top quality healthcare from folks who truly seemed dedicated to making lives better. At the time, I had no idea the healthcare workers taking care of Stu had to endure low wages and unfair working conditions like short shifts. I mean, it's criminal that a kid starting at Dunkin Donuts can make more than a professional healthcare worker at an assisted living facility like the Pines. But that's the America we live in today, where we prioritize the profits of corporations over the welfare of workers and their families, and where our government leaders actively try to suppress the labor unions who are defending those workers. The Pines is owned by a national corporation called National Healthcare Associates, Inc. in addition to many other facilities across the country. How does a union like 1199 SEIU force a huge corporation to the bargaining table? Really their only option is to develop some public outcry with informational pickets just like this one. The Pines is a popular facility in Poughkeepsie, but it won't be popular for long when citizens find out the workers taking care of their loved ones here are being treated unfairly.

I'm here to support these healthcare workers who are fighting for a better life. I'm also here for Stu – because he would probably want me to.

They are calling 2023 the Year of Labor, and for good reason. The number of workers in America going on strike this year increased 280% over 2022, including work stoppages at Ford, General Motors, and Kaiser Permanente, as well as the massive Writer's Guild and SAG strikes shutting down Hollywood.

Workers have successfully formed unions this year at Starbucks and Amazon, with places like Apple and Tesla not far behind.

The crowd outside The Pines is getting larger, with Rob Pinto bringing vanloads of reinforcements from Communication Workers of America (CWA) Local 1120 to support their union brothers and sisters in 1199 SEIU. Rob has been the Political Coordinator for CWA for twenty years, and he's also Vice President of the Hudson Valley Area Labor Federation (HVALF). He was born and raised here in the Hudson Valley as the son of teachers, so I think he's probably been fighting the good fight his whole life. I first met him at a Michelle Hinchey event, but it was a few months later at a Pat Ryan fundraiser in Kingston when he pulls me aside and says, "I've been organizing a long time, Tommy. And I've got to tell you, I've never seen a campaign like yours," he says, shaking his head. Then he cracks a big smile. "But I *like* it."

Thanks, big guy! I will take it as a compliment.

Back in June, Big Papa gives me the honor of delivering the keynote at the Democrats' annual Salute to Labor event. "On one condition," he says playfully. "You wear a jacket." The event is a big deal; it brings together all the local unions in the HVALF, from the New York State Nurses Association (NYSNA) to the International Alliance of Theatrical Stage Employees (IATSE) for an evening of community and of course, a chance to meet the Democratic candidates running this year. I work hard on writing my keynote address. And I do wear a blazer – the sparkly blue one from the county convention.

I start with a simple question. "Do you remember your first job?"

As you might expect with a hall packed with proud union members, I get a lot of great responses. They're shouting out their first jobs like we're on a game show. It's an easy way to get an audience on your side. (I've been doing the same thing with my Marist students for twenty years.) Then I ask, "Do you remember how you felt when you got the very first paycheck from that first job?" A burst of nostalgia follows, everyone talking about how good they felt as a kid earning that money, no matter how small. "That's the same feeling we wish for our kids today," I say. "But that wish is under attack by corporations who only care about their bottom line."

I go on to talk about my vision for a Dutchess County government that actually puts the welfare of working families above that bottom line of corporations. I talk about the county's Industrial Development Agency, or IDA, which is supposed to bring new business opportunities to Dutchess. The members of the IDA are approved by the County Executive. I tell them, "I think it's time we change the name to the Workforce Development Agency, don't you? Isn't building workforce housing a key element of attracting new business?" It's a radical idea, sure, but it's not an impossible one. And I also say, "I'm not promising labor unions a better seat at the table, like every other politician promises you each year. No, I'm saying: *we need a new table*. We need to build a whole new table, together." I end with a wonderful quote from Dr. Martin Luther King Jr. about the lasting power of unions, and the room erupts in applause. I've never met most of the people in this room, but by the end of the night, I will shake hands and speak with every last one, even as the event staff breaks down the tables and chairs at the end of the night.

"Great speech," Big Papa says as we walk out. "I picked the right guy for the job."

Another compliment? Whoa. Don't worry, I won't let it get to my head.

The sidewalk outside The Pines is at fever pitch with even more people joining the picket line, including Assemblyman Jonathan Jacobson. He's been supporting unions for so long they call him Uncle Jonathan whenever he shows up to say a few words; today I'm chosen to be his warm-up act. I'm getting pretty good at giving stump speeches with zero notice – practice makes perfect, I guess. I don't have to think too hard on what I'm going to say this time; with the crowd circled around me, I just start talking about Stu Vidal. As soon as I say his name, some of the union members who work at The Pines immediately start to get emotional, shedding tears because they remember Stu. (I'm getting misty, too.) I don't have to say much else. I just say, "The people who took such good care of Stu deserve better. They deserve a new contract. They deserve fair wages and better working conditions. Their voices deserve to be heard. And that's why we're here today, to support our brothers and sisters in labor and raise our voices with yours. Union Strong!" I get a lot of applause, as well as a flurry of whistle bursts from Yvette's boys.

Jonathan smiles and gives me a look that says, *how do I follow that?* He needn't worry, though. Before he even says a word, people are shouting "Uncle Jonathan!' from up and down the street. This is clearly his crowd. But I've had the best day. Yvette and I showed up early, and we stayed until the end. I forget she's been doing this for years. We had such a great time today, getting into some of that good trouble.

"You look happy," Yvette says to me, her two sleepy kids in tow as we head back to our cars.

I am beaming. "Honestly? This is the kind of stuff I wish I could do every day."

"When you win the election," she says. "You *can* do it every day."

I haven't heard from Devereaux since our first meeting, so I decide to bite the bullet and give him a call to remind him of his promise to help me raise $100,000. After buying our lawn signs, the campaign is desperately low on cash. We've done really well on individual donations, which is something I'm super proud of – but when your average donation is around $30, it would take years to fund big-ticket items like TV spots and prime billboards. We don't have years; there's only three months to go before election day. Our first filing in July revealed we are being outraised by a ratio of about 6:1, give or take. Not good.

I don't have Devereaux's cell number, so I ask Big Papa for it. I already have a good idea how this call is going to go – if he even picks up, that is. I'm fully expecting to leave a message when he picks up on the second ring. "Hello?"

"Hey, this is Tommy Zurhellen. How are you?"

There is a pause. "I am doing well. I'm watching this baseball game right now."

"I didn't mean to bother you. I just wanted to follow up on the conversation we had this spring."

"Yup." There is another long pause. "Like I said, I'm watching this baseball game."

"Okay," I say, already deflated. "Do you have any advice for me, then?"

"Yeah," he says. "Don't quit your day job." And then he hangs up.

It only takes me a few hours to get over the brief shock of being treated so rudely. I figure he's been following my campaign and has winced at all the "bleeding heart crap" I've been championing, like food insecurity, homelessness, and labor unions. I assume he changed his mind, without telling me. When I talk to Big Papa and Amelia, they confirm my suspicions.

"Well, he might think you're too progressive," Big Papa says diplomatically. I get the idea he's known this for a long time before sharing it today, but I don't say anything.

Amelia tells me Devereaux basically did the same thing to another Democratic candidate running last year: he promised the moon at first. But later he went missing, presumably because he didn't agree with some things on their platform. That's interesting, because I had lunch recently with the last Democrat to run for Dutchess County Executive, to pick his brain about the campaign. He's a nice guy named Joe who's been involved in Dutchess County politics for a long time. When I tell him my Roger Devereaux story, he laughs.

"What's so funny?" I say.

Joe has a bitter smile, like he's feeling an old wound. "Let's just say, it sounds familiar."

When I started this journey back in February, I probably would have accepted any money thrown at me, just because I didn't know any better. But now it's August and I can see how this weird underworld of politics works much more clearly now. I wouldn't feel right accepting money that has strings attached. Could the campaign use $100,000? Of course. But I value my self-respect a lot more than that. We've come this far with hard work and a positive message. And I would choose the message over the money, any day.

Around the same time I talk to Devereaux on the phone, I have a Zoom interview with a local grassroots climate group, hoping for their endorsement. I think the interview goes really well; it's clear we agree on a host of issues including shutting down the trash incinerator, ending the lead pipe crisis in Poughkeepsie, and even finding a way to put a dedicated bike lane on Route 9, the main north-south artery in the county. But a week later I receive an email from the group saying, we are not giving you our endorsement. Basically, the email says I'm not progressive enough.

You're too progressive. You're not progressive enough. I think people are looking for their perfect candidate, the one that checks every single box in their minds. The problem is, that candidate does not exist. When you withhold support from a candidate because they don't match up to the perfect candidate you have in your head, that's dangerous, because you're just helping the opposing candidate to win. For me, Democrats are so wonderful because we are so diverse. Yes, diversity is our greatest strength. We are all so beautifully different and yet we share common goals of social justice, equality, and freedom. We're all supposed to be working together for real change. But that's near impossible when some folks hold back support merely because they are waiting for their own perfect candidate to magically appear, year after year.

It ain't going to happen.

I might not look like it to you, but I am the perfect candidate on the ballot this year! Anthony Parisi, Kenya Gadsden, Jim Rogers and Yvette Valdes Smith are also the perfect candidates this year. Why? Because we're the only candidates who are running in Row A! The alternatives on Row B are so much worse. I mean, stuffing homeless folks in the jail? Spending $25 million on improving a baseball stadium when thousands of kids are going hungry at the same time? Allowing international corporations to lease county parks instead of letting residents enjoy them? Yikes. Anything would be better than that. I wish more people saw it that way – but sadly, they don't. I think sometimes we narrow our vision instead of looking at the whole picture and understanding the needs and passions of everyone, not just our own. Which might be a perfect definition of kindness.

Okay, I am now stepping down from my soapbox. On with the show. I mentioned some important environmental issues a moment ago, and it reminds me of another interesting parallel to Dante's *Inferno*, now that we have made it all the way down to the Seventh Circle of Hell. (Only two levels left to go! Time flies when you're trying to escape the underworld, I guess.) The Seventh Circle is reserved for those who have committed sins of violence; the interesting part for me is the way Dante prioritizes the different kinds of violence he sees in his world, 700 years ago. All violence is reprehensible, of course, but according to the poem, the worst offenses are violence against art and nature. For those who committed violence against nature, their fate is living under a rain of fire instead of cooling water. The idea of nature probably held a different definition for Dante than it does today, but I still like to think that this old poem foresees the disaster of man-made climate change we are facing in the 21st century. Will shutting down the county trash incinerator move the needle when it comes to global climate change? Probably not. But it will reduce the abnormally high rates of asthma reported in kids living in the neighborhoods adjacent to the incinerator, I can guarantee that. Will finally replacing the lead pipes that deliver Poughkeepsie's drinking water help to cool the planet? Of course not. But it would mean thousands of kids in our community would not be exposed to lead, which can cause a myriad of mental and physical health issues in young people. We've heard it before: think globally, act locally. I believe we can all do our part to make the world a better place to live, for future generations. I haven't had the chance to talk about environmental issues in this book until now, but I want to make it clear that I've been stumping these issues and more on the campaign trail. They might not be issues that big-dollar donors like Roger Devereaux care about, but they're things I care deeply about.

Okay, now I am stepping off the soapbox, but for real this time.

Lawn signs are in! Even better, they're going like hotcakes. I've been waiting for this moment since February, to hold my very own lawn sign gently in my arms. It's a rite of passage for every candidate. They are five dollars' worth of corrugated plastic and steel wire, but until now I had no idea how important they are in political campaigns. I probably get the same question ten times a day: "Are your lawn signs in yet?" People sure want to stick them in their yard! Well, most people. But the jury is still out on whether lawn signs can actually help a campaign, especially today in the age of social media. Many pundits maintain that lawn signs don't vote, only people do. But in 2010 a study at Vanderbilt University named the "Ben Griffin" experiment threw a wrench into that logic. In the experiment, lawn signs for a fictitious county council candidate named "Ben Griffin" were placed on lawns near a local school. Then a questionnaire was sent by the school's PTA asking respondents to rate their choices for county council. Seven candidates were listed, including Ben Griffin, who was in the top three picks for a quarter of the people who responded. The study concluded that in races where little information is available, lawn signs could be very important.

The general rule of thumb for a good lawn sign seems to be, the simpler, the better. Too much information on your sign means people driving by won't see anything. So, for my signs, I decided to make the TOMMY as big as possible, because that's really all a voter in Dutchess County needs to know. If they already know who I am, they don't need any other information. If they don't know who I am, I figure their first question is going to be, "Who the Hell is Tommy?" and they will find the answer on social media. Either way, I win. I do add "Veteran for County Executive" at the bottom, because my veteran status might be an important detail for some. Overall, I'm proud of the design of these lawn signs, which I have Nora to thank for as usual, whenever it comes to our visual media design. She's designed everything from our t-shirts to our monthly event calendars to the layout of my weekly email blast, all of which have become immensely popular with folks who have joined Team Tommy. We haven't gone with any other traditional campaign swag like buttons or pins, simply because we can't afford them on our shoestring budget. (By the way, my teammate Kenya has some great campaign pins, for sure! They are in the shape of sparkly eyeglasses, reminding us to "see" our world from a different perspective. Genius!)

I didn't know lawn signs could be so expensive! Five hundred two-sided outdoor, multi-color signs with wire stands will run you $2500 or more, depending on the vendor. For my signs – and all of my printed campaign materials – Ted and I agreed early on we'd only buy from union shops. Ted located a union printer in Albany that's also a woman-owned business, so it was a double win in our book. Sure, our signs cost a little more than the quickie online vendors, but it's worth the extra money if you support labor unions like we both do. And the signs look a lot better, too.

I drive up to Albany in my truck to pick up our first batch of 500 signs and stands. They're all gone in a matter of days, but we have to wait a while until we can scrape up enough money to order a second batch and later, a third batch. I absolutely love this Little Campaign That Could, and I love seeing new TOMMY signs pop up outside homes all over the county, especially in towns and neighborhoods considered Republican strongholds. There are many more GO SUE GO! and VETERANS FOR SUE signs out there, but they're mostly recycled from her campaign for state senate last year, and we're slowly catching up. And I'm beginning to realize that for some Democrats in Dutchess County, depending on where they live, putting a lawn sign in their yard is an act of courage.

I'm still trudging through my call time these days, and even though I'm not seeing a whole lot of results, I always manage to find some memorable conversations. I speak with one woman in Fishkill, a registered Democrat, whose first question for me is, "Why don't I see any of your yard signs in my neighborhood?" She sounds angry, or at the very least, offended.

"I don't know," I say. "Would you like me to bring you some signs for your yard?"

"Oh, no," she says, her voice lowering to a whisper. "No, I couldn't do that."

"May I ask why?"

"Too many Republicans on my street."

That's just one example of the longtime, ingrained fear I'm sensing from so many Democrats as I travel around the county. Republicans have been in charge for so long, that fear gains a kind of muscle memory that lingers even today, when there are now officially 20,000 more registered Democrats than Republicans living in Dutchess. But you wouldn't know it, because year after year, that same fear translates into not putting your candidate's name on your lawn, simply because the Republicans on your street won't like it. Who knew a little lawn sign could be such an act of defiance? We can't keep our TOMMY signs in stock, which means there's a bunch of people out there hungry for real change this year. And that's an encouraging thought, especially for a guy being outspent 6:1 by his opponent.

I'm dropping by a potluck breakfast in Wappingers Falls to support some local candidates running for town council and supervisor. On the campaign trail, I quickly learn that "potluck breakfast" means there will be twelve different boxes of Dunkin Donuts, one jug of orange juice, and – you guessed it – a pan of pigs in a blanket, or something similar. I've also learned to always bring a box of coffee, because no one else does. Anyway, I'm enjoying some conversation with all three of my teammates and also answering a few questions from locals when a guy approaches me, wringing his hands. I don't know his name, but I know he's married to a woman running for something here in Wappingers Falls. "Do you have a minute?" he says nervously.

"Have a seat," I say. "What's on your mind?"

The man takes a chair across the table from me. "My wife told me I shouldn't bring this up," he says, peering across the room. "But I think it's really important, and I wanted to let you know my thoughts."

If this guy starts talking about dandruff, he's going to get a jelly donut to the face.

"Your lawn signs," he says. "I like them, but I think the lettering at the bottom is too small. I can't see the part that says, 'veteran for county executive.' And I think that's a big problem."

"Thanks for letting me know." I'd like to know his definition of a small problem. But I tell him the reasons why I think TOMMY is really the only part of the sign that's absolutely essential.

"Okay," he says slowly, considering my answer. "But are you going to change it to make the smaller print bigger?" This gentleman obviously has a passion for lawn signs.

"I really can't do that," I say. "We've already ordered 1,500 signs, and I think it's important to keep them all consistent." That's actually true. Later in the race, Anthony's opponent for District Attorney will run low on money to order more of his original signs, so he's forced to buy some ugly, single-color signs that look so cheap, they probably are losing him votes.

Listen, I will take a conversation with this guy any day over the next conversation I will have at this breakfast, which is with a MAGA guy trying to convince me he's not MAGA. But it underscores the fact that lawn signs might not decide an election, but they are very important to the people who want to support you. People want to plant that sign in their yard as a little beacon of hope. They want their lawn signs to signify a small but mighty act of courage. And for the amazing folks who are supporting me, I think they want my lawn sign to stand as a declaration that this year, they are choosing kindness over fear, even if I don't win the election.

We didn't come this far just to settle for some moral victory. Ted and I are both lifelong teachers, so we are used to making things work with macaroni and glue. But with less than three months until Election Day, it's becoming clear that without the funds to purchase TV spots or bulk mailers, we're going to need more than macaroni and glue to make up for it. We're going to need a miracle – or three – as we enter the home stretch. Next month, we have four debates lined up with my opponent, so that might be one opportunity to turn some votes our way. And three of the labor unions I met at the Salute to Labor – 1199 SEIU, CWA Local 1120, and the New York State Nurses Association, have agreed to come together, mobilize their members, and knock on doors to help the countywide candidates get out the vote this year. Will it be enough? Who knows. At least it won't be boring. I do know one thing for sure: I would much rather walk alongside my union friends than rub elbows and schmooze with big money donors, any day of the week.

All to say, if we are going down, we're going to go down swinging.

But wait. A rumor is going around, one I've heard from a few different people. Word around the water cooler is that Sue Serino's campaign has spent money on a proper poll. Scientific polls can be very expensive, which is why most local campaigns don't do them. We're talking tens of thousands of dollars. But the idea makes sense: there's only a few months left before this election, my opponent is flush with cash, and she's running against a guy with twelve dollars in the bank who won't go negative, ever. For Republicans, I can imagine it's worth the peace of mind to know how comfortable Sue's lead has become, so they can divert funds to other candidates not doing so well.

I know the rumor is at least half-true, because I happen to be one of the people who receive the poll in a text message. (For the record, I didn't respond.) The other half of the rumor is the juicy part: when the poll results come back – surprise! – they are a lot closer than what the Republicans thought. Now, I want to be clear that I cannot confirm this part of the rumor, even though I've heard it from separate sources. But I can verify that from this point on, Republicans will roughly double the money they are spending on this race. That's right. As of August, I'm being outspent by a margin of 6:1, which is embarrassing enough. But by Election Day, they will pile it on until that ratio widens to 12:1. Wow! Rumor or not, our Little Campaign That Could is obviously making somebody very nervous. I don't think anyone is more surprised than me. Call it what you want – a coincidence, an anomaly, a good old-fashioned red herring -- but I'm a hopeless romantic so I'll just call it a miracle. It's a miracle because somehow, we've managed to hold this thing together with nothing more than macaroni and glue, plus a positive message of kindness and inclusion. And if that's not some kind of bright magic at work in this dark world of American politics, I don't know what is.

Union strong! I'm standing in the parking lot next to CWA Local 1120's headquarters on the edge of Poughkeepsie, waiting for another miracle to happen. I'm here way too early, and I know it; I couldn't sleep a wink last night, tossing and turning with too much anxiety over how many people would show up on this cool Saturday morning. When Rob at CWA, the two Maurices at 1199SEIU, and Sandra at NYSNA all promised the four Democratic countywide candidates a combined, massive get-out-the-vote effort, honestly it took my breath away. This is exactly what we needed, at exactly the right time. When campaigns have a lot of money, they pay professionals to canvas for them; in this case, the candidates themselves might only knock on a few doors, just enough for photo-ops. (Strike a pose!) But when campaigns don't have money to spare – that would be us – they must depend on supporters coming out to volunteer in large numbers. These folks are only getting paid in donuts and coffee, as well as the satisfaction they're part of something important. So, when these amazing labor organizers pledged to gather their members from all over to descend on Dutchess County to knock doors for us, it felt like answered prayers. And right now, I'm standing alone in a parking lot, hoping those promises come through.

Early in the campaign, I received enthusiastic pledges of support from a whole lot of people – electeds, other candidates, political clubs, colleagues, friends – who offered to hold a fundraiser at their home, help with logistics, connect me with influential contacts, and so on. I call them "April promises" because they sure sound good at the beginning of the campaign, but by August those vows have dissipated into the wind. They were never real in the first place. I don't take it personally; after all, it's a wonderful way to find out who your friends truly are. But it's also made me more guarded and wary whenever people pledge their support to my campaign, especially when they promise the moon like my union friends have done. Call me doubting Thomas, I guess.

But I will learn a new lesson today: never doubt the word of labor unions.

This turns out to be a glorious day. Union members from all three unions are showing up in droves, wearing their colors and bringing so much energy and camaraderie. The parking lot filled up a long time ago; cars and vans are lined up and down the road in both directions, and I'm told there will be busloads to come. My teammate Jim Rogers and I are standing together, taking it all in. I'm pretty sure Jim is crying tears of joy underneath his sunglasses, and I'm not far behind him. I think we're both emotional because we realize all these people have shown up for us. They trust that we are worth fighting for. Before we all split up this morning to fly around the county like a mighty herd of butterflies, we take pictures together and share stories like we're at a family reunion. In a way, that's exactly where we are.

"Well, what do you think?" Rob says to me as we all begin to disperse. He's even brought his teenage son to help knock on doors today. "Are you impressed?"

"Impressed is not the word," I say, my eyes still wide with

wonder. "You brought the cavalry, and then some. I can't thank you enough."

"We're just getting started, brother. Don't worry, we've got your back."

I realize now those April promises I mentioned before work both ways. A candidate who makes promises but never backs those promises with action can never hope to gain trust. I'll give you an example: recently I visited an emergency meeting for the Hudson Valley chapter of the American Postal Workers Union. The meeting was called to discuss a response to the horrible news that Postmaster DeJoy had ordered several local post offices to close. The union had invited all local electeds and candidates to attend, but in the end, only three showed up: Congressman Pat Ryan, Assemblymember Jonathan Jacobson, and yours truly. Most people had no idea who the big fella sitting in the back row was, but I spent the whole time listening intently to the union members, and clapping like Hell whenever someone stood at the podium to tell their story. I didn't show up for a name-check or a photo-op. I didn't wear a name tag or fancy suit. I showed up because I want to support our unions any way I can, period.

Word must travel fast, because soon after that meeting, I get a call from a friend who is a member of the APWU. She tells me the union has voted to endorse my campaign, and they wanted to know where to send the official letter. Wow! Out of all the humbling endorsements I've received – from Planned Parenthood, Vote Vets, and many other incredible organizations – I have to say that letter from the postal workers' union means the most to me. I put it on my wall of my Marist office as soon as I receive it. The letter is special because it's proof positive that if I keep showing up to do the work, people will notice, and they will come to trust me. Nose, meet grindstone. It's a lesson my father tried to show me a long time ago. A lesson that labor unions are teaching me today.

Union strong! Sorry, couldn't resist one more.

EIGHTH CIRCLE

SEPTEMBER IS here, which means my freewheeling summer of campaign miracles has officially come to an end, now that school is back in session. (I didn't quit my day job.) There's two months to go until Election Day – we're rounding third and heading for home! – but once again, winning an election must compete with my teaching schedule, student conferences, reading student writing, and lesson plans – as well as all sorts of faculty meetings, which are another version of Hell. Before the summer break, my students had no clue I was running for office, and probably no interest, either. But it's a different ball game for the fall semester.

"Hey, professor," a student says excitedly as he walks into class a few minutes late and plops down into his desk. "I was coming to class, and I saw a sign on my street with your name on it. What's the deal?"

I rub my chin slowly, feigning ignorance. "Hmm. What did the sign say?"

He thinks for a moment. "I don't know. It's like, one of those political signs."

"Yeah, I saw one too," another kid says, and suddenly the whole classroom is paying attention, even the young woman texting under her desk and the young man nodding off in the back. "Are you like, running for something?"

I sigh and tell them I'm the Democrat for Dutchess County Executive. When I do, our reading of Billy Collins' wonderful poem "Introduction to Poetry" is utterly doomed, at least for now. They have many questions, and like most educators who have been doing this for a long time, I try to turn their budding curiosity into a teaching moment. We have a frank discussion about homelessness, food insecurity, and climate change. They're asking smart questions. Most students are interested, some are even shocked. They had no idea the homeless shelter stands only a few blocks from campus; they were also surprised to learn thousands of children in Poughkeepsie go hungry every day. That teaching moment must have made an impression, because my students will keep asking me for updates on the campaign right up until Election Day. A few even share that they will be voting for the first time this November, and they're excited about it. But this is a teaching moment for me, too, because I learn that my students are interested in their world, and their community. Talk to older Americans today and they'll all say something like, *kids these days, they don't care about anything.* That is not true. When I listen to my students, I realize they care deeply about certain issues, like climate change and sustainability. They care about kindness, in their own way. And that makes a teacher feel good.

I wish I could report that everyone at Marist has been as supportive of my campaign as my students, but that's not the case. I'm not the first faculty member here to run for public office, although you wouldn't know it with the way I'm being treated after twenty years of dedicated service. This semester, I will get called into my dean's office on a regular basis for a repeated warning not to use Marist in any way in my campaign. And I receive three different versions of a memo from Marist lawyers, explaining the same warning in more detail. I am told I cannot speak at the event I created, Anthony's Walk, which is a community walk held at Marist each September to raise awareness on veterans' issues.

And perhaps the cringiest decision of all comes when a student writes a piece about me in the student newspaper. Marist decides to add a disclaimer above her story in bold lettering. I mean, it's the *school newspaper,* people.

I feel so badly for that kid, I could cry.

At least I'm not alone. My friend Rebecca, who is a professor across town at Vassar College, tells me she is experiencing similar shenanigans. She is running for Town of Poughkeepsie supervisor, and she must be doing very well in the race because the opposition is running those demonizing ads on social media describing her as a (gasp) "liberal college professor." God forbid. Rebecca's opponent must be on a low budget because the black-and-white ads look exactly the same as those old 2016 spots demonizing Zephyr Teachout as a liberal college professor. (Remember those?) Anyway, don't worry, I'm not going to dwell too long on this sad little detour. I just want to say that it's hard enough trying to do my job at Marist and running for office at the same time, without the hassle. Has higher education changed since I started teaching? Yes, in many ways. The only constant for me has been the joy I feel helping students find their own way. Well, that and some students are always showing up late. But that's a whole different book.

For me, September is also going to be the start of "debate" season here in Dutchess County, so in my spare time I'm mulling over strategy and what I want to talk about. I put the word debate in quotation marks because since the very beginning of this weird journey, people have made it abundantly clear that my opponent does not do debates – as in, the kind where a moderator asks questions and candidates bandy words back and forth on the issues. Sue doesn't bandy, and I'm told she would never agree to a true debate where she might have to go off script. So instead, we have both agreed to take part in a total of four events where Sue and I will have a chance to speak in the same room. (Not very

Eighth Circle

exciting, I know.) I'm even less excited when I learn the first three debates will be hosted by the Mid-Hudson Mortgage Bankers Association, the Realtors Association, and the Dutchess Chamber of Commerce. I should mention that my opponent Sue Serino is a realtor. But I am willing to run the gauntlet of these three Republican-dominated organizations because the fourth debate is sponsored by the NAACP, and that's where I know I will be able to talk about the issues I care about. I have it marked on my calendar for October, and even though that's a month away, I can't wait. But first I will have to hold my own at each of those three GOP-friendly events, starting with the Mid-Hudson Mortgage Bankers Association dinner, which is being held at the Ship Lantern Inn across the river. Wish me luck.

I walk into the restaurant a few minutes late because I just got out of my evening class; I know they've already started because I can hear Sue's voice, talking about having "skin in the game." I had to dismiss my class early to get here, but in twenty years I've never had one student complain about that. Ted is already here, standing by the door with a clipboard – wishful thinking, cousin, since I doubt we will be picking up any new volunteers tonight from *this* group. The program for tonight is simple: Sue will talk for ten minutes, and then I will talk for ten minutes. Afterwards we're supposed to answer questions over dinner. The Ship Lantern Inn is one of those old-school fine dining joints that were popular in the 1960s but today if you're under the age of 75, it feels like a time warp stepping through the door. It's dark in here, and the warped wood floors creak like a Spanish galleon under my shoes. The lingering smell of Lysol and cigarettes reminds me of grandma's house. Which makes this the perfect venue for mortgage

The High Road

bankers and their spouses. This is prime Republican territory, for sure. The only way Sue loses any votes tonight is with a major flub during her speech, like losing her place in her cue cards.

I lean over to Ted as Sue is talking. "This place gives me the creeps," I whisper.

"Tell me about it," he whispers back. "I live down the street."

In my head, I'm counting the number of times Sue repeats the phrase "skin in the game" during her remarks. I think we're up to three or four since I arrived. Being an English professor and a general lover of language, I will say that there's a reason why we no longer use phrases in public like "peanut gallery," "cake walk," and yes, "skin in the game." These phrases (and many more) can be offensive because they are based in racism or bigotry. So, when I hear someone use a phrase like "skin in the game" in a speech, I want to let them know someone in their audience might be offended.

But then I look at the audience here tonight and I figure, maybe not. There are about seventy Trump votes in the room, dressed for Sunday dinner. Besides Ted, I don't know one person here – wait, is that Jonathan Jacobson sitting at a table in the back? Indeed, it is. What's he doing here? I guess his reputation for showing up everywhere is earned. We make eye contact, and he gives me a smile and a hopeful thumbs up.

Sue's getting close to the end of her time when she loses her place in her index cards. Full stop. She doesn't try to move on or go off the cuff. Instead, she sputters, flipping frantically through her notes, trying to regain the talking point she was supposed to deliver next. I don't look at my watch, but it feels like an eternity before she finally finds her place again, putting the train back on the tracks. Thirty seconds of dead air can feel like an eternity in public speaking, I know. Honestly, I don't care if we're supposed to be competitors, I feel so bad for Sue at this moment. I hope someone gives her a big hug after this event is over.

Flub or no, Sue gets a warm round of applause when she wraps up. Now it's my turn. I step to the microphone – no suit, no tie, no name tag, and definitely no index cards – so the MC can introduce me. And here is my introduction by the MC, in its entirety: "This is Tommy Zurhellen."

There is a smattering of polite applause. I look out at a grey sea of blank faces.

"Thank you for that wonderful introduction," I say. "I'm touched."

That earns me a few laughs from the crowd, including Jonathan Jacobson, who I have never heard laugh before. Thankfully, the room loosens up by a smidge – which is a victory, in my book. I should leave now while I'm ahead. But I dive into my stump speech, starting with the affordable housing crisis and what we can do about it. I'm proud to say I don't use any cheat cards or crib notes when I speak; it's common knowledge at Marist that my teaching philosophy has always been, *let's see where this takes us.* On the campaign trail, I think it's an advantage to be able to think (and talk) on your feet, rather than resorting to a set script. It gives you confidence because if you've done your homework, there's no question you can't answer.

In other words, it makes you fearless.

A few minutes into my remarks, I notice they are bringing out the salads and shrimp cocktails. I start talking about the homelessness shelter, and most of the faces turn away, intent on starting their meal. A woman in the back corner starts talking loudly to the woman sitting next to her. I've got a good five minutes left on my time, but it's clear the room is ready to move on. I'm talking about homeless people being forced to live in an old jail, and these folks just want to dig into their shrimp cocktail and enjoy their evening. Rude? Sure, but I'm used to it by now. I figure I'm not going to win many friends here tonight anyway, no matter what I do.

So, here's what I say next. "Listen, if you don't care about homeless people, then I don't want your vote." People are putting down their shrimp forks. That sure got their attention. I say it again, even louder this time. "If you don't care about homeless people, *I don't want you to vote for me.*" Whoa, even the chatty old lady in the back corner is silent now. I am catching a lot of shocked glances and open mouths from all over the room. I don't look in Jonathan's direction because he's probably got steam blasting out of his ears. "Do I have your attention now?" I say, and there are a few slow nods.

I talk for another couple minutes about food insecurity and thank them for their time. There's more applause now than when I started. But in a few seconds I'm out the door and breathing cool evening air under the neon Ship Lantern sign in the parking lot, with Ted right behind me. He watches me pace in circles for a few moments.

"You want to go back inside for the dinner?" he says, still holding the clipboard.

"Nah, cousin. I think I lost my appetite."

He nods. "Tough crowd. You sure woke them up, though."

My hands are shaking. I'm on edge, but not because of what I said to them about caring about homeless people – heck, I'd say it again, every day of the week, because I really do feel that way. No, I'm angry with myself for breaking the first rule of public speaking: never let them see you sweat. But I'll get over it. Later that night, I get a surprise voice message on my cell from Jonathan Jacobson. He's not yelling at me this time. "Hey Tommy, it's Jonathan. I thought you did pretty good tonight. You got their attention, that's for sure. Why did you leave? There were some people who wanted to talk to you. Anyway. I just wanted to tell you, good job. Keep it up."

Wow, did Jonathan Jacobson just give me a genuine compliment? I think so. He didn't even mention the lack of a name tag.

Things are looking up. But the degree of difficulty only gets higher now, with the second debate at the Realtors Association contact breakfast. There will be a lot more people, and it will be a lot closer to an actual debate, with a moderator, time limits, rebuttals, and all that jazz. But Sue is a realtor; this will be her home turf. So if I want to steal this one, I'll have to come up with a brand new strategy to do it.

I'm not the only candidate walking through the debate minefield these days. All three of my countywide teammates Anthony Parisi, Kenya Gadsden, and Jim Rogers have their own cases to make against their Republican opponents. Each has their own NAACP debate scheduled for October, but in addition, Anthony has an earlier debate sponsored by the D.A.'s office, to be held at the Stabilization center. His opponent for Dutchess County District Attorney is an old guy named Matthew Weishaupt who has been in the D.A.'s office for 36 years now. He's the handpicked successor to current D.A. Bill Grady, the Republican who is stepping down after 40 years; that's a long time for two men to control an office – any office. Since the Stabilization center is directly across the street from Marist, I walk over after my last class to catch the debate and support Anthony.

From my perspective, it's a lopsided affair. Anthony is clearly the more articulate and experienced candidate. When the candidates are asked about what changes they want to bring to the D.A.'s office, Anthony is like a laser, talking about modernizing the outdated computer system, bringing intelligence-based policing to the county, and adding a conviction integrity unit, which would investigate wrongful convictions involving a felony. That sounds important to me, but as it turns out, Dutchess County doesn't even have a conviction integrity unit.

His opponent's answer on what changes will he bring to the D.A.'s office? "I want to add a Facebook page." As always, Anthony comes off well-spoken and *damn*, this guy knows his stuff. He's really worked on being more comfortable and confident in front of a crowd since that first meet-and-greet we shared in Pine Plains. In contrast, his opponent comes off as a rambling mess. But I notice something else during the debate: Anthony is getting increasingly irritated over something as the event continues. Towards the end, his answers are clipped and a little less focused, as if he's distracted by something. I look across the room at Sinead who is standing by the wall, arms folded, and she looks irritated, too. What's going on? The moderators end the event when it hits the 90-minute time limit, which means there's no time for the promised audience Q&A. I wait a few seconds for the crowd to disperse before going up to the podium area to congratulate Anthony and Sinead on a great debate, but they've already exited the room. I don't find them in the hallway, either. I go outside to the parking lot and I see Sinead with her arm around Anthony's shoulder, like she's consoling him. I step closer and I notice he is shaking. Honestly, I've never seen Anthony as emotional as this before.

Sinead is even more livid than her husband, and as I understand it, this debate was a set up. Some of the pre-set questions were changed without telling Anthony, and the moderators apparently made some other changes to the format without telling him, too. Whatever was done, Anthony seems convinced he lost the debate. That's not true, of course, but it's hard for him to see it that way right now. As his teammate, it's my job to keep him focused, the way my teammates have done for me so many times on the campaign trail.

"Come here, big dog," I say, taking him aside as people stream out the door into the balmy night air. "Did you hear a guy in the back laugh out loud when your opponent said, *we're going to get a Facebook page?*"

"Yeah," Anthony says, breaking a smile.

"That was me." We share a quick laugh; at least he's stopped shaking by this point. "Listen, Anthony, they're desperate. You're the better candidate, and everyone knows it. You're going to win, but they don't want to admit it. So, they're going to throw every dirty trick in the book at you, trying to get your goat. Why? Because that's all they can do. It's all they have left. You've got less than two months to go. Just keep your cool, okay?"

"I will," Anthony says. "Thanks, Tommy."

When I announced my candidacy, veteran candidates like Kenya and Yvette told me stories about the Republican bag of dirty tricks in Dutchess County. Honestly, I thought they were making them up, or at least exaggerating a bit to spellbind a political novice like me. But I'm here to say, they are all true. I was told Republicans drive around in a van at night to steal their opponents' lawn signs, which sounds far-fetched; but each morning, I do find some of my signs missing, and Anthony, Jim and Kenya all report the same. Still, I'm thinking it could be the wind, or an aggressive lawn mower. That is, until the news breaks in October that a Republican candidate in Fishkill was arrested by police for stealing his Democratic opponent's lawn signs; the case wasn't too hard to solve, since he kept them in the back of his SUV and garage.

It wasn't the wind, after all.

Stealing yard signs is just the start. One of my favorites is the scary but vague form letter they are sending out, warning everyone that if you vote for a Democrat, then Dutchess County will be less safe. The letter doesn't offer any proof, of course, and it looks like it has been photocopied so many times, you can barely read it; I'm guessing the original version was written sometime in the 1990s, judging by the dot-matrix printing. It's not signed by anyone. It's just an anonymous scare tactic meant to make people afraid, but the letter itself is so grainy and amateur it's probably doing the opposite. Ugh. I imagine there's a dark room with no windows where "operatives" go down the annual checklist of dirty tricks. Steal lawn signs? Check. Photocopy and send threatening letters? Check. Change the rules of a debate and don't tell the Democrat? Double check. Change the venue for a public event at the last minute and don't tell Democrats that, either? Triple check. What a sad life these people must lead. I should count my blessings, though; I haven't been a direct target of their bag of dirty tricks.

At least, not yet.

Round two. The Dutchess County Association of Realtors (DCAR) contact breakfast is being held at the Villa Borghese, which is one of those old-school wedding halls with marble floors and gold chandeliers every suburb in America has tucked away somewhere. If you say you live in Dutchess but haven't been here at least once for a bat-mitzvah, quinceañera, wedding anniversary or retirement shindig, you're either lying or you drank too much champagne to remember it. I've been to the Villa Borghese so many times I've lost count; I was here just a couple months ago to support Kenya and her wonderful charitable organization, Les Souers Amiables. Lots of fond memories here. None of which are helpful as I walk through the doors, scan the cavernous banquet hall, and quickly realize I don't know anyone here – not even Jonathan Jacobson. There's a guy setting up the sound equipment up front who must have noticed me staring like a lost child, so he comes over and introduces himself. He looks around the room. "Where's your entourage?"

As a joke, I check my pockets. "It's just me."

"Really?" he says, surprised. He motions to a table on the other side of the hall. "Sue brought hers."

"Naturally," I say, peering over at Sue's table to wave hello, and she waves back. Sure enough, Sue's table is filled with family, her campaign manager, her assistant campaign manager, and a couple of college-aged kids I'm assuming are interns? I don't know. Either way, there's a genuine pre-game tailgate going on over there.

The sound guy returns to his set-up duties. "Sit anywhere you want, I guess."

I take a seat at an empty table up front and start drinking glass after glass of ice water. On my third pour I get a soft tap on my shoulder; as it turns out, I do know someone at this thing after all. It's my friend Matteo, who's a Democrat running for a seat on his local town board this year. He's a stylish young fellow sporting a ponytail and dragon tattoos – at first glance, not exactly the type I'd expect to see at a realtors' convention. But he's a realtor nonetheless, and I'm so glad to see a friendly face – maybe too glad, because I stand up and bear-hug the guy like he's picking me up at the airport. "What are you doing here, Matteo?"

"I was about to ask you the same thing," he says, looking over at Sue's table. "You're a brave man for showing up here." He grits his teeth. "I wouldn't do it."

"Thanks for the confidence boost, man."

"No problem. But seriously, I don't think you have anything to gain. This is her territory."

"You're not helping, Matteo." But I tell him to come find me after the debate is over, to see if I've changed his mind at all.

After a few minutes of DCAR announcements about upcoming events, we get straight into the debate. I'm standing behind a podium looking out at a few hundred people, which is a big step up from the gaggle of old folks at the Ship Lantern Inn. It's a different crowd, too; I see some younger people and people of color. The MC introduces Sue and I and then we give our opening statements, with Sue going first.

When my turn comes, I start with a joke. "Wow," I say, wiping my arm across my forehead. "Taking on Sue Serino at the realtors' association? I might as well be debating Derek Jeter at the Yankees convention, right?" The line gets big laughs, and I can feel the temperature go down in the room already. "I'll just have to do my best."

My strategy today is simple: put people at ease. Most of these folks are meeting me for the very first time, but they have undoubtedly heard about my fiery stances on things like the homeless shelter and hungry kids in Poughkeepsie. They are expecting a large, angry social justice advocate to show up and lambast them on not doing enough for their neighbors in need, right? These are realtors; they are expecting to tune out right away.

So, from the start I give them something they don't expect: a funny, down-to-earth, regular guy you wouldn't mind having a beer with.

In other words, a big sweetie.

It's a gamble, but the big sweetie strategy pays off. I don't have any note cards or memorized bullet points in my head, so I'm just bouncing off things Sue is saying, trying to find humor without forcing it. As I expected, all the questions are directly related to realty codes and property management. There's not going to be any questions about homelessness at the realtors' convention, which is the way I want it. I'm no expert when it comes to property management, for sure, but I don't have to be – by now, I've done enough homework to know what I'm talking about when it comes to wonky things like the unfairness of Fair Market Rent (FMR), the reasons behind the increase in REO (Real Estate Owned) properties, and the county's Industrial Development Agency (IDA). And I can see a lot of surprised faces in the audience when I stop to correct the MC on some minor terminology when he asks us a question about the new Short Term Rental Registration Law that will go into effect this September.

Surprise, surprise! This big sweetie knows his stuff.

Another piece of my strategy for today is to make it clear Sue and I have always been friends, not enemies. I refer to her as "my friend Sue" at least a dozen times and even when I want to show a marked difference between us, I use a soft pivot and say something like, "I have to gently disagree with my friend Sue. Let me tell you why." Above all, I don't want to come off as the villain today, especially against someone as well-liked as Sue.

We're over an hour into this thing, and people at the tables are getting restless, checking their phones. The MC says, "Okay, question fourteen –"

I interrupt him. "Question *fourteen*? Geez, how many questions you got in this thing?" My joke gets another big laugh from the crowd, because they're obviously thinking the same thing. Am I pandering to my audience? Oh, you bet.

The MC shrugs his shoulders. "Okay, we'll make this the last question," he says, and some people start to clap and cheer. I hear one woman in the back shout out, "Thank you!"

Our last question is about a proposed New York state law that would make it more difficult to sell family farms for other purposes, like shopping malls or housing developments; he asks us, are we for or against this law? Being a big sweetie is fine, but I also need to draw a line between me and Sue before time is up. Sue goes first in her response and it's clear she is strongly against the law. "I mean, if someone wants to sell their farm and move to Florida, I say, why not?"

I take my chance to draw that line; when it's my turn, I slowly shake my head. "Well, Sue, I don't know how things are down in Florida," I say, as if I'm offended. "But here in Dutchess County, I can tell you there are a lot of people suffering with the affordable housing crisis. I live in Poughkeepsie. Anyone else here live in Poughkeepsie?" A dozen or so hands shoot up, and I point to the closest one. "Then you know what I'm talking about. We're in a crisis, and we're all in it together. Call me crazy, but I just think we need a County Executive who cares about what's going on right here at home." I pause for effect. "I don't really care what happens in Florida." Did I answer the question? Absolutely not. But when I look over my podium at the end of my time, I see a lot of heads nodding.

It's time for closing statements and as I am speaking, I notice there are two people at Sue's table writing every word I say down on paper. There's no video or audio recording allowed at the debate. As I finish my closing remarks, they're still writing away. They must have been doing it the whole time, and I'm not sure why.

The event is over, and I feel good. My big sweetie strategy worked as well as I could hope. So many people are coming up to congratulate me, there's a little bit of a receiving line. Matteo stops by on his way out. "You proved me wrong," he says. "You did well. You made people laugh. I think you surprised them."

Whew! I don't have time to pat myself on the back for a job well done because I have office hours at Marist in a few minutes. Two debates down, two to go. The next one is hosted by the Dutchess County Chamber of Commerce, which means an even bigger crowd. It will take a whole new strategy, because I don't want to give them the same look as today -- but it's worth it, because I'm looking forward to the scheduled NAACP debate in October. As I drive back to Marist, I'm still wondering why Sue's people would be furiously writing down every word I uttered at the Villa Borghese. I will find out, soon enough.

While we're waiting for the next debate, I'd like to take a moment to clear the air on something that happens up in Pine Plains right around this time in September. My friend Chris Drago, who is running for Dutchess County Legislature to represent Pine Plains and Millerton, as well as his beloved Aunt Fee will be especially interested, I think. This story takes place on a sunny Saturday at an outdoor tiki-type bar; the four countywide candidates have been invited to say a few words at a social event sponsored by the Pine Plains Democrats. The outdoor bar is split into two distinct halves: the bar area up front, and in the back, a fenced-in lounge area that has tables and a little raised stage. We're in the lounge area, and it's a good turnout of local Democrats, many wearing Chris Drago t-shirts. I'm standing back by the bar, munching on chicken wings and waiting my turn to go up to the mic and deliver my usual stump speech. As soon as the event starts, however, there are some rowdy gentlemen sitting at the bar who are getting vocal, spouting the usual Trumpish nonsense. I'm not sure if the Democrats in the lounge area can even hear them, but I sure do. The barflies are getting louder and bolder, so I confront the one making the most noise, trying my best to be kind. "You're being mean," I say to him, but when he turns to face me, it's obvious the guy is drunk or high – or both.

His buddy tries to come to his rescue, but it becomes a half-hearted attempt when he realizes I'm three times his size. "Uh, he's not being mean."

"He *is* being mean," I say. "And he's going to stop."

That puts a stop to the shouting, at least for now. It's my turn at the mic, after Kenya – obviously the Pine Plains Democrats have not heard of the Kenya Rule, which states you never, ever want to follow a great orator like Kenya Gadsden at the podium – so I get up there to give my boilerplate remarks. But that confrontation with the jerks at the bar a moment ago has stirred something inside me. Man, I hate bullies. I want them to know these Democrats are no longer frightened of bullies like them. So, I call an audible and ditch my usual stump speech. Instead -- and to the surprise of everyone, especially my teammates – I ask the crowd to do a little call and response with me. I'm getting a lot of puzzled looks, but most folks are game for some audience participation. My goal is to make some noise, so the bullies in the back get a taste of their own bitter medicine.

Yes, I make it up on the spot. I ask the group to practice clapping like they're summoning a waiter at the Waldorf Astoria (clap, clap.) Louder, people! (*Clap, Clap!*) Ok, here we go!

My name is Tom! (*Clap, Clap!*) I am a veter-ahn! (*Clap! Clap!*)
Republicans don't know what the HELL is going on! (*Clap! Clap!*)
All right? (*Clap, Clap!*)
All right! (*Clap, Clap!*)
All right? (*Clap, Clap!*)
All right! (*Clap, Clap!*)

I do a couple more verses about my teammates and Chris Drago, all with the same basic cadence. I don't remember the words I come up with, but I do remember they don't rhyme. By the end, It gets pretty loud – and I have to say, after some initial poo-pooing by some, the crowd gets into it. Even Aunt Fee is getting pumped up. When I'm done, I step off the stage to warm applause. The only person not smiling is my teammate Anthony Parisi, because he is following me at the mic.

"Thanks a lot, buddy," he says. "How am I supposed to follow that?"

I think after today our Kenya Rule gains a small amendment called the Tommy Rule; namely, don't follow Tommy at the podium because who knows what that guy is going to do next.

I bring up this story now because I have the feeling people like Chris Drago and the Pine Plains Democrats believe I did it simply on a carefree whim. That is not the case. I did it because I wanted to teach those rude boys at the bar a lesson, without having to punch them in the face. And Chris, if you're reading this part, I hope you will share the story with Aunt Fee and let her know I wasn't trying to cheapen your event.

Clap, Clap!

Round three. We're in the main ballroom at the Poughkeepsie Grand hotel for the Dutchess County Chamber of Commerce debate. It's early on a Wednesday morning, which means I'm probably going to miss delivering my weekly veteran segment on WPDH radio as part of the Boris & Robyn show. Luckily, my partner-in-kindness and good friend Christa Hines has agreed to sit in my place and talk about our VetZero programs at Hudson River Housing, just in case this thing goes late. I've been to the Chamber contact breakfast once before; early in the campaign, my friend Jill invited me as her guest to do some networking. In return for her kindness, I promised to include her hometown of Dover Plains in the debate this morning – which isn't too hard, since Dover has its share of problems after years of neglect by the county; they've been without a grocery store for years now. The Poughkeepsie Grand is located smack dab in the middle of downtown Poughkeepsie, so it will be easier to talk about things like homelessness and food insecurity, since these issues are happening right down the street.

When I was here with Jill for the contact breakfast several months ago, the event was well attended, but the number of attendees has easily doubled today for the debate. They must be anticipating a show. And this is a more diverse crowd than the realtors' event; although most of the room is still staunch Republican, I see some diehard Democrats here, too, including my good friend John. Sue and I meet with the Chamber president in a side room to pick the order of the debate and go over the rules. Sue wants to go first with her opening remarks, and I relent as usual. This will be less of a true "debate" than the last one, since there will be no rebuttals and they've added something at the end called the "lightning round" of questions, where we can only give one word, yes or no answers. Sue and I both raise a worried eyebrow on that one.

Let the games begin.

As we are both introduced, Sue clearly receives the greater applause, including one guy standing up and shouting, "We love you, Sue!" But that's expected. I'm used to being the underdog by now. Many people here are meeting me for the first time. My goal is to receive more applause at the *end* of the event – and if I do, I'll know I changed some minds this morning.

My opponent goes first with her opening remarks, and immediately I realize why her people were writing down every word I said at the last debate: the talking points she's reading off her cards suddenly sound a lot like mine. Her ideas about affordable housing sound especially familiar. It's a dirty strategy, but an effective one; since Sue is going first, if I deliver my usual talking points afterwards, it will look like I am copying her ideas. As Sue speaks, I'm sitting at the other end of the dais, smiling. I'm not smiling to put on a brave face. No, I'm smiling because their strategy has a tragic flaw: little do they know, I'm not delivering any talking points today.

And now for something completely different, as Monty Python might say.

Now it's my turn. I start with some self-deprecating humor, and I get some solid laughs. As they loosen up a little, I do a quick U-turn. "Raise your hand if you're excited about putting homeless folks in the jail," I say to the crowd. I see a lot of shocked and embarrassed faces. Nobody raises their hand. "Anyone?" Still nobody. "Okay, raise your hand if you're excited about spending $25 million on a baseball stadium when there are thousands of kids right down the street here in Poughkeepsie who go hungry every day," I say, pointing to the doors behind them. There are hundreds of people stuffed in this room, and not one raises their hand – oh, wait, there is one. Sitting up front is the current County Executive Bill O'Neill, and he meekly raises his hand halfway. I point to him. "Let the record show that Bill O'Neill thinks a baseball stadium is more important than feeding our kids."

Ouch. Bill hangs his head. The room is completely silent now.

"Then what issues are we debating here, people? If we all agree we don't want to stuff homeless folks in a jail, what are we even talking about? And if everyone in this room cares about kids in Poughkeepsie more than luxury boxes at a ballpark – sorry, everyone except Bill here – then what do we have left to debate? Listen, if this race is just a popularity contest, I'm going to lose." I point at the guy who shouted *we love you, Sue!* at the beginning of the event. "Is this just a popularity contest to you?" I pause, but only for a split-second. "And if it is, don't we all agree that's pretty sad, when there are real problems facing our community, right outside that door?" Wow, the room is still silent. "I think we can all do a better job, together. Why not start today?"

Time is up for my opening remarks, but the damage has been done. Judging by the astonished faces, I'd say no one has spoken with raw frankness like that at the Dutchess County Chamber of Commerce, ever. The rest of the debate is less newsworthy, although I can report that Sue and I both agree the "lightning round" at the end is a disaster – neither of want to simply answer *yes* or *no* to the increasingly complex questions they ask us, so it quickly becomes a farce. "I'm really enjoying the comedy portion of the program," I say in the middle of it, which gets more laughs from the audience. After the event is finally done, I don't have much time to stick around and talk to people, because I have a string of faculty meetings at Marist. But I feel very good about my performance. I managed to surprise people, once again.

Later in the day, I get an email from my friend John who was at the debate. This is what he writes: *Hi Tommy. On my drive home I reflected a lot about the debate this morning. You provided blunt answers and even more blunt honesty, and you mixed in the right amount of humor; your Mom line killed. But I really wanted to share what I noticed, which I think matters most. When Frank introduced each candidate Sue received the more enthusiastic audience response. Forty-five minutes later each candidate made their respective closing remarks and that earlier tilt for Sue wasn't there. I don't have an "applause" meter so I can't prove my observation, but I know I am right. I think you moved the dial a bit in your direction. No small accomplishment when you are playing on the opponents' turf.*

It's been exhausting, trying to hold my own at each of these three Republican-friendly debates, but now I'm able to reap the benefit: the last debate is sponsored by the NAACP and held at the Cunneen-Hackett Arts Center in downtown Poughkeepsie. These last three events have been on my opponent's home turf, and I've had to play by their rules. But the NAACP civic engagement event will allow me to talk more about the issues I want to talk about. It will also force my opponent to talk about those same issues, in front of an audience that's a lot more diverse than a bunch of mortgage bankers or realtors. I'm so excited for that moment, and I'm preparing for it.

But sadly, that moment will never happen. Days before the event is supposed to take place, NAACP officials inform me Sue has backed out. She will not be attending their civic engagement event. There are conflicting accounts of exactly what happens, but I'm going to believe the NAACP. "They just ignored us," one NAACP official tells me. I am crestfallen, but I'm even more sad for the local chapter of the NAACP. I guess we should have seen it coming; after all, Republicans have been ignoring Black and Brown communities in Dutchess County long before this election, and they're going to keep doing it as long as they are still in power.

But as my Mom says, *when life gives you lemons, make vodka. Lemonade.* So, the event turns into a Q&A forum with one candidate for County Executive. The moderators and I have a good discussion on issues like institutional bias and community policing, but I have to say, it's lonely sitting up on that big stage at Cunneen-Hackett alone. The audience is small but engaged; I know most of the people here, because this is my city, too. At the beginning of the forum, a NAACP official reads their prepared statement on Sue Serino backing out of the debate with no warning; the statement leaves no room for discussion on the reason why she's not here tonight.

Honestly, this slight feels much worse than all the other dirty tricks our opponents have pulled. I can take the sign stealing, the idea stealing, and the scary letter sending. Greasy kids' stuff, in my opinion. But this feels like utter disrespect, not only towards me but more importantly, to the NAACP. After going through their three "debates" in good faith, I feel cheated. And upon reflection, it seems likely this was their strategy all along, never intending to subject Sue to an event clearly outside her comfort zone. Ugh. After this election is over, I plan to take a shower for at least a month, just to wipe away all the slime and muck plastered to my soul after trekking through this shameful, scummy underworld. I have a newfound appreciation for people like Amelia and Big Papa, who have to put up with it, year in, year out. I'm just passing through this weird, mean-spirited subculture on a nine-month tour; Amelia and Big Papa choose to live here, and I believe that takes a great deal of courage (and a whole lot of body wash.) Why does politics have to be such a mean business? Republicans seem to pull out the same bag of dirty tricks every year, with no consequences. To me, it all feels like a constant shell game, or a never-ending scam. It feels like fraud.

For my generation, perhaps the most powerful urban legend is what happens when you synch Pink Floyd's album *Dark Side of the Moon* to the classic movie *The Wizard of Oz*. (If you grew up in the 70s or 80s like me, you are bobbing your head like Wooderson right now and mumbling *all right, all right, all right*.) This legend makes perfect sense for a generation that has smoked more pot while watching TV than any other, by far. (Sorry, millennials.) Anyway, if you've ever tried starting Pink Floyd's album when the MGM logo comes on the screen, you know there is truth to this legend; a lot of things seem to be connected in more than mere coincidence, like the movie going from black-and-white to technicolor the second the song "Money" starts to play, or a heartbeat playing on the record as Dorothy listens for the Tin Man's heart. The band Pink Floyd has repeatedly denied the connections as nonsense, but that's not the point. The point is they do exist, whether they were put there on purpose or not. It's called serendipity. People celebrate these unexpected synchronicities precisely because they are *not* planned; it's probably the closest we can come to seeing magic in our daily lives – with or without the weed.

We're getting close to the end of our own journey here on *The High Road* as we now depart the Eight Circle of Hell and crossover to the Ninth and final stop on this journey through the underworld of American politics. Before we do, I want to take a moment to talk about how our story of running for office has synched up with Dante's *Inferno:* in other words, my nine months on the campaign trail compared to Dante's description of the nine levels of Hell. In writing this book, I must admit the comparison initially felt like a gimmick, and not very organic. But now as we get close to the end, I have to say I've witnessed serendipity much like synching Pink Floyd with *The Wizard of Oz*. Take the chapter we're in right now, the Eighth Circle of Hell. In Dante's *Inferno*, this level of the underworld is called Malebolge, which translates to "evil trenches." According to the poem, it's an immense cavern

Eighth Circle

with trenches carved into its walls, with each trench housing sinners guilty of all different kinds of fraud: hypocrites, flatterers, and yes, corrupt politicians. For the politicians, their fate is being thrown into a river of boiling tar and tortured by demons with grappling hooks, which gives you a little hint on how the poet Dante Alighieri felt about shady politicians in his world. When I started writing this book, I had no idea my eighth month on the campaign trail would connect to Dante's eighth circle so well. But that same kind of serendipity has happened too often not to mention it. And if you've made it this far in reading *The High Road*, you have likely noticed some uncanny connections, too.

I bring this up now because I'm beginning to understand how Dante's world 700 years ago must have worked in very similar ways to the world we live in now. Politics was a dirty business back then, just as it is today. Some politicians in Dante's time were fraudulent, just as some are today. Who knows, maybe fifty years from now, bored kids will be smoking weed while reading both Dante's *Inferno* and *The High Road* at the exact same time, but I doubt it. I mean to say, I doubt the reading part, not the weed.

NINTH CIRCLE

I'M SITTING in the back row of the auditorium at the old Poughkeepsie Day School once again. If you remember, this is the same place we officially launched this journey back in February when our slate was endorsed by the Dutchess County Democratic Committee (DCDC). Wow, that feels like a lifetime ago. Now it's October and we're all back for the DCDC Caucus, which is a last chance for party members to regroup and connect before a final push towards the election. There are only a few weeks left before Election Day. I don't want to be here, which is why I'm hiding in the back again. I'm not 100% sure I'm *supposed* to be here, either; I just got out of class at Marist and to be honest, I'd much rather be sleeping or finding something to eat that doesn't come from a drive-thru. But I'm here mostly because I don't want to disappoint Big Papa. He's been such a steadfast supporter and defender of my campaign – especially now, when a lot of people are complaining out loud about me refusing to take the turn to Negative Town and go after my opponent.

The caucus starts and after fifteen minutes it's becoming clear I don't have to be here, after all. There's no room in the agenda for any speeches from candidates, just busy work. Big Papa is up on stage, asking for updates from each local committee on what they're doing to get out the vote in their community. (Important work, for sure, but it's work that probably doesn't require the candidate for County Executive to be present.) As a result, I am about to make my exit, stage right, when a woman sitting down front stands up from her chair and waves her hands, trying to get Big Papa's attention. He stops the proceedings and recognizes her. "What can we do for you?"

She puts her hands on her hips. "Well, I want to hear what Tommy has to say."

Shit.

So much for that hasty exit. I really should develop better hiding skills. But I also admit hiding is difficult when you're a guy built like a walk-in freezer.

"Okay," Big Papa says, motioning a hand towards me. "Tommy Zurhellen, our candidate for County Executive – come on down!" I think he would make a pretty good game show host. I amble down towards the stage. I don't have the energy for any fiery speeches; heck, I don't even have the energy to climb the seven steps up to the stage, where Big Papa is waiting patiently to hand me the microphone. The people in the audience tonight are the same people who saw me for the first time on this stage back in February, when I fired them up with talk about "good trouble." That guy was a force to be reckoned with! But they are seeing a different guy now. A guy who is bone tired.

I slowly make it up to the stage and take the mic from Big Papa. I don't have anything inspirational to share with the few hundred folks staring back at me. I deliver some watered-down talking points from the campaign trail, but it's nothing special. I'm utterly exhausted, and I look it. Honestly, I just want to go home. I'm about to hand the mic back to Big Papa and do just that, but a man shoots up from his seat. "Will he answer questions?" the guy says, as if I'm a talking bear brought on stage for entertainment.

"Sure," I say with a sigh. But I know what's coming.

"When are you going to take the gloves off with Sue Serino?"

The High Road

the guy says, getting worked up. "You always talk about kindness this, and kindness that, *blah blah blah*, and that's fine. That's honorable, I guess. But it's not going to win an election against Republicans in this county. And I think a lot of people in this room feel the same way," he says, looking around. "So, my question for you is, when are you going to start attacking your opponent and expose her?"

The whole auditorium goes silent as I take a deep breath. "In a word? "Never."

I want to choose my next words carefully, but I also don't want to waste my energy trading words with another angry fool. These days, I get this question a lot. Secretly, I wish my grandma was here so she could take the mic to scold this guy and explain that kindness doesn't cost extra. But it's just me up here tonight, and I suddenly feel very alone. I remember something Amelia said back in February; she told me, running for office will be the loneliest experience of your life. Standing on this stage, I think she's right.

Yvonne Flowers has asked me to introduce her at the fundraiser she's having at River Station on the Poughkeepsie waterfront. Yvonne is the Democrat running for Mayor of Poughkeepsie, and if she wins, she will become the first Black mayor in our city's 200-year history. Amazing! I think *when* she wins sounds more appropriate, since Democrats outnumber Republicans in Poughkeepsie by a wide margin, and her opponent is an ex-cop who said, "I don't see color" at their NAACP debate this month, sparking a loud chorus of jeers and boos from the audience, including me. Yvonne's father is a bonafide legend in Poughkeepsie for his incredible philanthropy and kindness over decades of public service to the community, and Yvonne has gained quite a reputation herself for fighting the good fight as a member of our city council. I'm honored and a bit surprised she's asked me to give her introduction at the event; I know she is longtime friends with my opponent, Sue Serino. But I have a strong reputation within the City of Poughkeepsie for helping others, so it's a smart move. Pretty much everyone knows the "big guy in the funny hat" by now for helping veterans and our homeless neighbors, and more.

We're on the second floor of River Station, a restaurant with beautiful views of the Hudson River, and plenty of city residents and other Democrats have come to support Yvonne, including my teammate Anthony Parisi and his wife, Sinead. With only a few weeks to go, Anthony looks about as tired as I am. Assemblymember Jonathan Jacobson is here, too. For my remarks, I decide to rely on a bit of nostalgia, in the form of a history lesson.

"I've lived in the city of Poughkeepsie for twenty years," I say, after name-checking all the electeds and Democrat candidates in the room. "I love my city. But it's changed over the years, hasn't it?" I see a lot of nods out there. "I remember my heroes, the people who stood up for Poughkeepsie back in the day. People like Barbara Jeter-Jackson." As soon as I say the name, the room fills with love, everyone wanting to talk about this local legend and longtime county legislator who passed away a few years ago. I tell them my own Barbara Jeter-Jackson story, where she invited me to the Dutchess County legislature to present me with an award for walking across the country. "And people like Tree Arrington." More love, as the crowd fondly remembers the larger-than-life advocate who helped countless kids in the city, and who also passed a few years ago. Then I tell them my Tree Arrington story, about sitting in his office at R.E.A.L. Skills Network and talking about food insecurity in our city. "These people are my heroes. They will always be heroes to me," I say. "But now Poughkeepsie needs new heroes. Heroes like Yvonne Flowers." Now the room erupts in applause. I talk about Yvonne's father, and about Yvonne's own impressive work in the 5th Ward. "Now, allow me to introduce *my* hero, and our next Mayor of Poughkeepsie, Yvonne Flowers." Yvonne gives me a big hug as I step away from the microphone and walk towards the back of the room.

"Good speech," Jonathan Jacobson says as I pass his table.

"Thank you," I say. Maybe it's the lack of sleep, or the fact that I have now received *two* compliments from Jonathan Jacobson, but whatever the reason, I'm feeling a little giddy. "Wait, does that mean I'm a *coachable* candidate?"

"I don't know about that," he says with a wry smile. "But it was a good speech."

About a week later, I'm speaking at another fundraiser and Jonathan will come up to me afterwards, nodding his head. "You're getting pretty good at this," he says, which is about the best compliment an old pro like Jonathan could give a novice like me. "I'm going to donate to your campaign," he says, pulling out a checkbook from his pocket. I won't remember the amount, but to me, it doesn't matter if it's ten bucks or ten thousand. I feel like I'm finally getting a bit of respect for all the effort I'm showing as I try my best to win this election, doing it my way. Yes, his check means more than a donation to me, at this point. It means respect; respect I've earned by showing up every single day and outworking almost everyone on the campaign trail, no matter how much money we have in the bank. I'm proud of that.

We're coming down to the wire. It's a soggy Saturday morning in October and as usual, I'm trying to fit as many events as I can into one weekend. Kenya's idea of the "Two Tommys" has multiplied into three or four, with the madcap pace I'm setting for myself as I try to meet as many voters as I can before Election Day. This morning, I'm starting with an event in Poughkeepsie called the Walk for Freedom, with the purpose of drawing attention to the global crisis of human trafficking. It's sponsored by a local nonprofit organization. Campaign or no campaign, I would be here to support this event; as a board member at Grace Smith House, this is an issue very close to my heart. After the walk, I'm driving down to southern Dutchess to accept an award for community service from the Union Vale Democrats. I think I've got three more events Ted has put on my Google calendar for the rest of the day, for a total of five. My record for events attended in one day is seven – and that's with a strict "no photo-op" rule in place: if I am attending an event, I'm going to engage the event as best I can, instead of merely stopping by to take a photo, as most politicians do. (I know my friend and teammate Yvette Valdés Smith follows the same rule, because she's the one who taught it to me.) It takes a lot more effort this way! But I wouldn't feel right doing the usual hit-and-run.

The Walk for Freedom starts at Waryas Park on the Poughkeepsie waterfront. It's raining but there's a covered stage and a good crowd gathering for the event, despite the damp weather. Sue Serino and her entourage are already here when I arrive, and as I peruse the program, I see she's one of the featured speakers. Wonderful. I see some friends from the community, and we chat for a few minutes under our umbrellas and wait for the event to start.

As I mentioned before, this event is sponsored by a nonprofit; one of the organizers gets on stage to introduce the first speaker. "I want to introduce to you the next Dutchess County Executive, Sue Serino!" she shouts into the microphone. "She did a wonderful job as state senator, and she's going to do an even better job as our County Executive. I can't wait until she takes office and see all the great things she does!"

Um, what? Hey people, I'm standing *right here.*

Sue gets some warm applause as she takes the mic and starts into her remarks. She doesn't acknowledge me, or the fact that the election hasn't been decided yet. Her entourage looks on with stone cold faces, ignoring my presence. They know as well as I do that Sue's introduction wasn't just mean-spirited -- it was illegal. Campaign laws in our state don't allow any 501(c) nonprofit organization to show favor to any candidate – just ask Marist, who wouldn't even allow me to speak at my own event. I stand there for a few moments, dejected. If I felt alone in that auditorium at the Poughkeepsie Day School last week, I am feeling even more alone right now.

Keep it together, underdog.

When I get to the awards ceremony hosted by the Union Vale Democrats, there is a dark cloud hovering over my head. I can't shake it. I should be used to it by now, I know. In a few minutes, I'm supposed to be accepting the Gertie Strum Award for community service – the hundred or so people in attendance are going to expect a funny, cheerful speech as usual from their champion of kindness, Tommy Z. My friends Heidi and Mike Tucci of the Union Vale Dems worked hard to build this event, and I don't want to disappoint them. But I can't seem to mask my intense sadness. My brain is going in a million different directions. For so long, I've been the guy who always shares kindness with others. I desperately need someone to return the favor and share kindness with me. And I need it now.

As if on cue, my teammate Kenya Gadsden walks in the door. She and her husband Bernard have come to support me, and I couldn't be more grateful. "You don't look so good," Kenya says, putting a hand on my shoulder and taking me aside. "What's wrong?"

I tell her about what happened that morning at the walk; I think she can tell I'm in no shape to give an acceptance speech right now. "I got you," she says immediately. "Go sit down next to Bernard and have something to eat. I'll take care of this." She finds Heidi and Mike Tucci and after a short conversation, there's a small change made to the event program: Kenya Gadsden will deliver some remarks right before the award presentation, which takes the pressure off me to do much more than say, "Thank you."

She hasn't prepared anything of course, but Kenya gives us an amazing speech about kindness and service that only Kenya could deliver. After the event, I can't thank her enough for stepping in and saving me like that.

"I'm just returning the favor," she says. "You carried me when I was out with my hip replacement. Now it's my turn to carry you."

Kenya's act of kindness at the Union Vale Dems event has got me thinking about the reasons why I feel so lonely, especially with only weeks left to go in the campaign. I don't have an entourage following me from event to event, and I don't want one. Maybe I've been too exhausted to see it, but I realize now that I've had so many people rooting for me and finding ways to support me the whole time. Kenya stepping in for me at the awards ceremony. Sinead *still* tying my shoes. Costa at the Eveready donating the whole cost of my breakfast event at the diner, just because he likes my message of kindness and inclusion. Michelle at the gym offering subtle encouragement after the step class, even though I'm obviously a hot mess. The Fiancée making trays of kale salad and spinach lasagna for my fridge, because she knows I'm not eating well. My oldest friend Jeff calling from NYC every week to check in and listen to me complain; Christa doing the same with our weekly Friday beer summit. Big Papa making time to attend every event, even though he's probably busier than I am. I could go on for a whole chapter (or two) recalling the ways people have returned kindness to me, a hundred-fold. If I focus on that instead of dwelling on all the cruelty and spitefulness I've experienced on the campaign trail, the world looks so much brighter. I've always believed kindness brings kindness in return, but only in theory; now I am seeing it in action. And it's going to get me through.

The ending of Dante's *Inferno* is not for the faint of heart, and it's definitely not rated PG-13, either. To escape the underworld, Dante and Virgil must crawl down the genitals of the Devil himself. (I am not making this up.) At the bottom of Hell, Satan is trapped in the middle of a lake of ice, with his huge, grotesque torso and bat wings exposed above. The only way out is a small crack between the ice and the Devil's furry – um, junk. I'm guessing the Prince of Darkness hasn't had a chance to freshen up down there in a while. Dante and Virgil shimmy down feet-first, but when they do they reach the center of the universe (what a trippy medieval poem, right?) which means gravity shifts in the opposite direction; to keep going down, our heroes must now climb up. In other words, their world is turned upside down. At first, Dante panics because he thinks the 180-degree change in direction means they are headed straight back down to Hell. (Whoa! Totally disoriented? The world turned upside down? Right now, I can second that emotion.) But Dante's trusty guide Virgil talks him through the ordeal and the dynamic duo finally emerges to find a beautiful, starry sky above, putting an end to their epic journey. Here's the last few lines of Dante's epic poem:

> *The Guide and I into that hidden road*
> *Now entered, to return to the bright world;*
> *And without care of having any rest,*
> *We climbed up, he first and I the second,*
> *Till I saw the night sky through a round aperture*
> *And all the beauteous things that Heaven holds.*
> *Finally, we came forth to behold the stars again.*

Dante has made it all the way through the underworld, completely exhausted but unscathed. I am imagining the fear and frustration he must feel at the end of his quest; he's so disoriented, he can't find the way out. I'm also imagining his incredible relief and gratitude when he finally gets to gaze up at those stars and breathes fresh air for the first time since his journey began.

Like Dante, I am on the very last leg of my own journey. I feel completely disoriented, too. Now it's my turn to scramble up the last hill and find my way out.

It's Election Day in America and I'm standing on a street corner in Rhinebeck, New York holding a handmade sign that reads VOTE FOR A VETERAN TODAY. It's 6am and I think I have misjudged how early people in the Hudson Valley get up for work, because right now the streets are completely empty, except for me and Nora. But traffic will pick up soon. I hope. Nora is waiting patiently on the opposite corner with her iPhone, hoping for a good photo of me with the sign. But 6am in chilly November means it's still too dark for photos. (Yes, I should have thought this one through a little more.) I should have planned on bringing coffee, too, because I'm so tired, I'm having trouble standing up for more than a few minutes at a time. I can't believe it will all be over in a matter of hours. I'm determined to leave it all on the playing field today. Will these last-minute theatrics make a difference in the vote count? Who knows. But that's not the point. Win or lose, I don't want to wake up tomorrow, wondering if I could have done more. I don't want to let down all the people who have rallied around this Little Campaign That Could.

After a day toting this sparkly sign all around Dutchess County, I head to the Poughkeepsie train station to meet the last commuter trains coming back from New York City, reminding folks there's still time to vote before polls close at 9pm. I lost my voice days ago, so my words come out like sandpaper. My friend Brooke from Spectrum News texts me, hoping to get a last-minute interview before the polls close; I've known her since she covered my walk across the country for Spectrum, four years ago.

Brooke sets up her tripod camera right in the middle of the train platform, a few minutes before nine o'clock. When we're done with the interview, she becomes the first person to ask me a question I will get frequently in the months to come. "Now that you're done with the campaign, which was more difficult? The walk across America, or running for office?"

I think for a moment. "This has been more difficult. It's not even close."

She's surprised. "I would've thought the opposite."

I tell Brooke the walk was easy when I figured out why I was out there in the first place. Everyone was so kind along the way, even total strangers. I woke up every morning *wanting* to keep walking, because it meant meeting more forgotten veterans along the way and listening to their stories. "I've felt more alone running for office than I ever did during the walk."

She's finished breaking down her camera. "Would you ever do it again?"

"Do you mean walk across America, or run for office?"

Brooke smiles. "Either. Both."

"Neither," I say. "But if I had to choose, I would do the walk, every time."

I walk with Brooke back to her car and she stuffs the camera case into the trunk. She wishes me good luck tonight before she drives away into the night. I really want to go home and collapse into my bed instead of driving over to the Pirate Canoe Club to wait for the election results, but I don't. I owe Nora, Ted and all my teammates at least that much. They are all just as tired as I am. As I slide into my pickup truck, I sit there in silence for a few moments. For the last nine months, this truck has been my campaign headquarters, executive dining room, emergency bathroom (don't ask) and communications center – not to mention, my designated crying/moaning area when things don't go so well.

God almighty, it smells absolutely terrible in here.

I crack the window. The visor above my eyes has about a hundred HELLO, MY NAME IS stickers layered like a leaf pile – together, they serve as a brief history of a political campaign, nine months spent on a strange journey through a dark and frightening world. The passenger seat is covered with stacks of postcards and palm cards, along with plenty of fast-food wrappers and my laundry – some of it clean, some dirty, some downright toxic. No wonder it stinks in here; how have I not noticed the stench before? I've saved two Tommy lawn signs for myself and they're jammed in there, too. I don't turn the ignition right away; no, I'm not changing my mind about the Pirate Canoe Club. I just want to sit here for a few minutes and try to process things for the first time. What a long, strange trip it's been. In the darkness of the train station parking lot, I say a little prayer for myself. I'm hoping I come out on the other side of this thing unscathed, just like Dante. And I'm praying I can hold it together as I await my fate, waiting for my own return to the bright world, already knowing I will have a new appreciation for the beauty of the stars once I see them again.

Epilogue
RETURN TO THE BRIGHT WORLD

JANUARY 2, 2024

It's a beautiful, crisp winter day as we gather at the Cunneen-Hackett Arts Center in Poughkeepsie to witness the swearing in ceremony of the Honorable Anthony P. Parisi, our new District Attorney for Dutchess County. The room is filled with what looks like every peace officer, prosecutor, parole officer and public defender working in the Hudson Valley – if there's a perfect moment to plan a bank heist, this is it. I'm sitting next to my friends Kenya Gadsden and Jim Rogers as we wait for the festivities to begin. I haven't seen any of my former teammates since election night, and it's simply wonderful to catch up with Kenya and Jim as we laugh and reminisce about the journey we took together. The tone of our conversation is bittersweet; we are beyond excited to support Anthony and celebrate his victory, of course, but I also think we still share a lingering taste of vinegar from our own defeats, two months ago. All three of us lost, but not by much. Jim only lost his race for Family Court Judge by a handful of votes, and Kenya got much closer in her rematch for County Clerk – an incredible feat, considering she was out of commission for a stretch while recovering from hip surgery. As for me, I lost my race for County Executive against Sue Serino – but it was a lot closer than anyone imagined, including myself.

Up on stage, Sinead has her hands full with her two young

daughters, but she manages to slip away for a moment to say hello to her old running buddies. It's so good to see her, and Sinead's ebullient smile tells me she's the most relieved person in the entire room. We all know Anthony would not have won without her. Naturally, Sinead tries to assess my shoelace situation, but they are hidden underneath the chair in front of me; she's still in den-mother mode, and I love her for it. "How's the shoelaces?" she says.

I pull one foot out. "Slip-ons," I say. "It's a New Year." She looks impressed.

The dignitaries take their places on the stage, and we're ready to begin. Overall, the ceremony itself is fairly standard – well, all except the Pledge of Allegiance, which is wonderfully led by Anthony and Sinead's daughters, from memory. As the event nears its end, there are more than a few misty eyes in the room, including mine. (Luckily, Kenya always carries tissues in her bag.) I'm getting emotional for a few reasons; first, I know just how hard Anthony and Sinead worked to win this election, and I'm happy for them as they begin their new adventure. Anthony will be the first Democrat in at least 100 years to hold the office of District Attorney in Dutchess County, and it will mean a complete sea change when it comes to fairness and justice in our county. The days of old-boy politics in the D.A.'s office are finished. I know Anthony will do a great job. I'm also crying because I was part of the team that helped him reach the mountaintop. A flood of memories rushes through my mind. The camaraderie we earned picking each other up, day after day – that will be the hardest thing to let go. I might have lost my election, but I have gained lifelong friends I know I can always count on. And that's worth more to me than anything.

After Anthony takes the oath of office and the event is over, I am losing count of the number of people coming up to me to say how sorry they feel for me since I lost my race for County

January 2, 2024

Executive. They're surprised to see me out in public, as if I've been a hermit, avoiding people for the last two months (not entirely untrue.) But they're even more surprised when I tell them, I'm not sorry at all. Honestly, I'm excited! I tell them, Democracy is a team sport, and overall Democrats won an amazing victory in Dutchess County in 2023. In Poughkeepsie, we elected the first Black mayor in the city's history. We gained three seats in the Dutchess County Legislature (including a win by Chris Drago!) which eliminates the Republican super-majority and their ability to pass legislation behind closed doors. We also turned the Town of Poughkeepsie blue, gaining a 4-3 advantage on the town board thanks to Rebecca Edwards' win in the race for town supervisor. Democrats in the Town of Stanford enjoyed the same victory up in northern Dutchess.

Sorry? No way. Clearly, we have plenty to celebrate!

Nobody likes to lose, of course. But I am so proud of what we accomplished in the race for County Executive, because we raised awareness on issues like food insecurity, affordable housing, and the homelessness crisis. And that awareness will yield tangible results: in 2024, the county government will announce a new program to fight hunger in our kids and abandon the horrible idea of housing our homeless in the old jail. When we started, hardly anyone in Dutchess County knew what "food insecurity" was, and even less people knew about the county's plan to stuff the homeless in the jail. That's progress, for sure.

For me, life has largely returned to normal in the New Year. On top of my normal teaching duties at Marist, I always have plenty of work in the community to keep me busy; the only difference is, I don't have to take pictures and send them to Nora to post on social media anymore. I love the work I do. I'm still delivering the evening meal for the homeless shelter, collecting essential items for places like the Dutchess County SPCA and Grace Smith House, and helping to raise funds for worthy projects – including adding an access ramp to Liberty Station, the veterans' shelter in Poughkeepsie. When the election was finally over, I thought I would have a lot more free time, but that's not the case; I'm still just as busy, but now I'm back to doing the work I truly love, and that makes a huge difference.

    I still drop by the Eveready diner for breakfast a couple times a week. Felix and the boys are much the same, roosting on their stools to drink coffee and talk sports and politics, although one member of the crew in his 80s has been going through rounds of chemo recently. We try to cheer him up whenever he feels strong enough to come out to the diner. And I still manage to get to the gym twice a week for that same step class; I'm still in the back row, but I'm no longer hiding. Michelle and I have become good friends, and thanks to her encouragement, I'm finishing the whole 40-minute class these days without collapsing. Baby steps. By now, most folks in the class have learned I'm the guy who walked across America *and* wrote a book about it. (I suspect Michelle might be behind that, too.)

    As you might expect, I receive a lot of invites for Democrat events, and I do make time to attend a few, here and there. When I show up, most people seem happy to see me, but it also feels weird, as if I'm a retired gladiator sitting up in the bleachers while the genuine warriors are down in the arena, doing the things I used to do. And besides, not everyone at these things is glad to see me walk in the door; I think I made more than a few people angry last year when I wouldn't go negative, or wear a nametag, or talk about the issues that donors expected me to talk about. Seeing those same people now can be, well, awkward. But awkward or not, I will always be proud of everything we accomplished in our campaign last year. Looking back, I think I'm most proud of never backing down from that original promise to run a campaign based on kindness. So many people laughed and jeered when I told them I was running a campaign based on kindness. And so

January 2, 2024

many more people wrote me off when they realized I was never going to waver from that promise, even at the end. They expected me to lose, and lose big. But even though we were outspent by a wide margin by the end of the campaign, we managed to earn 44% of the vote. That doesn't happen without a great deal of hard work, passion, and creativity. I know we did the very best we could with the resources available to us.

I believe we achieved a victory much more important than winning an election, because our campaign disproved the notion that politics has to be the nasty, cutthroat business we see on TV. In his 2017 book *Across That Bridge*, civil rights icon John Lewis gives us fair warning when he writes, "Political parties are on the hunt to search and destroy each other, as though we were involved in some kind of enemy combat, rather than the work of statesmanship. Campaigns have become a free-for-all of dirty tricks, scandalmongering, and distracting negativity that obscures the people's need to examine a candidate's voting record and see where he or she actually stands on the issues. I find myself asking, 'Why do we have to be so mean?'"

I am convinced there are partners in kindness everywhere. You just have to look.

So, can you win an election in America with kindness? I believe it's possible! Sure, we lost the race for Dutchess County Executive in 2023, but we also got a lot closer than Democrats did four years ago with a more traditional candidate. That's a comforting thought. We didn't have the money, but we clearly had the message. I think we proved a political campaign doesn't have to resort to scare tactics, dirty tricks or negativity to connect with voters. We proved that a positive message could engage voters more than the usual news of anger and fear. The election is long over, but people still come up to me in the grocery store and share how inspired they were by our underdog campaign, and that feels like a win. People always ask, "Will you run again?"

Never say never, I guess. But I've learned enough lessons from this rodeo for a lifetime.

Sequels are tough to write. Writing *any* book is tough enough, but trying to write something that follows a worn trail already blazed is especially difficult. Off the top of my head, I can't name more than one or two sequels I enjoy as much as the original – looking at you, *Empire Strikes Back* – and I think the reason has to do with the impossible weight any sequel has to bear. The story has to remind the audience of the original, but it must surprise them at the same time, offering something new and unique that sets it apart, on its own merits. That's a difficult balance to achieve; damned if you do, damned if you don't. Which is why most sequels, um, stink. For every *Empire Strikes Back* that perfectly captures the rare magic of the original, there are hundreds of *Meatballs II* or *Indiana Jones and the Last Temple of Mediocrity* out there that don't. (Sorry, Spielberg.) Did you know that Frank Baum wrote sixteen follow-ups to his novel *The Wizard of Oz*? Yeah, me neither. All to say, there's tremendous pressure when you're trying to write something that follows a story most people already love.

In 2020, I had so much fun writing *The Low Road: Walking the Walk for Veterans* because I got the opportunity to relive each day I traveled across America, meeting amazing veterans and listening to their unique stories. I felt blessed with the opportunity to experience the kindness of so many strangers on the road, one more time; I really didn't have to figure out the story, because the story was already there as I recalled each day. I didn't set out to write a book about kindness with *The Low Road*, but it sure turned out that way. And that made it an easy book to write.

It was much more of a struggle writing the book you hold in your hands, *The High Road: Following the Campaign Trail for a*

January 2, 2024

Kinder America. I think part of that struggle is derived from this book being a sequel, which I expected. But another reason I did not expect was *The High Road* being a different kind of story altogether. In many respects, this has not turned out to be *The Low Road 2* at all. This was a much more complex story, and I found it difficult to decide what to keep in the book or what to leave out, because this time around there were so many stories to choose from. Still, completing a book is its own reward, whether it was easy or not. I believe the more you have to work at something, the more it feels earned – and for a writer, that might be the best feeling of all.

Perhaps my favorite reward from writing this book is the fact that someone reading this right now might be thinking, *hey, I could do that*. I could run for local office and champion the causes I'm passionate about in my community. Maybe that someone is you! I hope my journey in *The High Road* inspires others to get involved and pursue a life of service. It doesn't matter how old you are, or how much money you have to spend. All you need is a good heart and a sturdy motor inside you that pushes you to help others, every day. If that describes you, I think you should start now! Contact your local party committee and tell them you want to serve your community by running for office next year. Trust me, they will be ecstatic about meeting patriots with passion. As John Lewis writes, "Who will emerge at the forefront of this struggle in the 21st Century? Perhaps it will be you." I can tell you running for local office will be hard work, but I can also tell you it will never be boring.

Speaking of sequels: what's next for me? What will I do for my third act, and my next adventure? That's a good question. On my birthday this year, my Dad tells me I should walk across the country backwards, but he's joking. (I mean, I think he's joking.) And every time I see my friend Chloe, she encourages me to answer the daily emails I get from the Peace Corps, to see if anyone could

The High Road

use an old, broken-down college professor and Navy veteran in other parts of the world. That would certainly be an adventure to remember. This year marks twenty years I've been at Marist. I love working with my students, but I also know I can't do it forever. Long term, I have no idea what I will do next, but I can tell you one thing about adventures: once you've had a couple, you tend to want to keep having them.

In the short term, I know I want to do everything I can to support my good friend and partner-in-kindness Yvette Valdés Smith this year in her race for a critical State Senate seat. She had my back last year, and now I want to return the favor. Thankfully, she is outpacing her opponent in campaign donations, something I could never do.

I'm strolling through the air-conditioned aisles at Stop & Shop looking for dinner ideas when I receive a gentle tap on my shoulder. I turn around to face an older gentleman sporting a grey beard and a Vietnam Veteran ballcap. He has a serious look on his face; I'm holding a box of cheesy mac and a family bag of chicken nuggets, so I hope this won't be a lecture on my lack of healthy choices, even though I need one. "Excuse me," he says politely. I notice he is wringing his hands. "I don't mean to bother you."

"You're not bothering me, brother," I say, waving the nuggets in the general direction of his ballcap. "Thanks for your service. And welcome home."

He gives me a quick nod, as all veterans do when someone says that. Then he pauses for a moment, still wringing his wrinkled hands, as if remembering a speech. "I want to say, thank you for all you did last year. Someone needed to bring up all the things you did, and I was proud it was a veteran like you. I know you fought like Hell. I know you didn't win, and that's a shame. But I

January 2, 2024

just wanted you to know there's a lot of people who are proud of you, and who care about such things. And I would be honored if I could shake your hand."

We shake hands with a firm grip. Honestly, I think I'm about to cry.

"Thank you," he says one last time and motors down the aisle towards the front doors of the store. I've never met this guy before. I don't know his name. And judging by the lack of groceries in his hands, I don't think he was even shopping here today. I get the feeling he prepared that speech months ago, anticipating the day we ever crossed paths. I stand there frozen for a while, clutching my horrible food choices, my heart overflowing with gratitude. Fifteen seconds of compassion from a stranger in Stop & Shop has suddenly made nine months of drudgery in the underworld feel like it was worth it.

For a book about kindness, I can't imagine a better ending than that.

AFTER/WORDS

My favorite part of *The Low Road* wasn't anything I wrote; for me, the most engaging stories came in the After/Words section, where I invited other people who appear in the book to share their own perspectives, in their own words. Whenever I pick up that book I go straight to the After/Words section, because those stories remind me of how every experience is shared. When it came time to write *The High Road*, I knew from the very beginning that I wanted to include an After/Words section again. I hope you enjoy listening to these voices as much as I do. They are not listed in any set order of importance, since they are all equally important to me. But since this is a book about kindness, I'd like to start with my friend and partner-in-kindness, Yvette Valdés Smith.

YVETTE

Picture this ... it's March 2023, the beginning of campaign season. Many of us in the county legislature were running for reelection and hoping to no longer be in the super-minority of only eight Democrats out of 25 legislators here in Dutchess County. We were working and fighting hard for the change we all deserve. We had seen the Republican super-majority waste taxpayer dollars on pet projects like funding baseball stadiums when we all knew we had real needs in our communities that were not being addressed. We knew that 2023 would be a challenge but between our work and the higher Democratic voter enrollment, we were hopeful.

It's always a process to find strong candidates to run for office. And we were excited when we heard that none other than Tommy Zurhellen would be our County Executive candidate. I couldn't wait to meet him. I had heard about the "big guy in the funny hat" for a long time. He's well known in our parts – the beloved, witty professor who founded VetZero after walking across America to raise awareness on veteran suicide and homelessness. His service for others has changed and saved lives. I knew we could win with Tommy. I had been serving as the Minority Leader of the Dutchess County Legislature and knew how much we needed a strong candidate and advocate for the people, like Tommy. As a mom of two young kids, former public-school teacher, and proud union member I was especially happy to have another educator among us.

The first time I met Tommy, we immediately started talking about expanding veteran services and what we could do for the young people of our county. It was always clear to me that he put others before himself. And I would think, "This is the change we need here in this county. He's the real deal." Then one day a couple of weeks after we met, I opened my mailbox to find a copy of *The Low Road*. He had inscribed it, *To my friend Yvette – Thank you for helping our heroes! – Tommy, USN*. He was a Navy man, just like my grandpa. I read his book twice and still keep it on my nightstand. His work, his words, and his actions inspire.

We all ran solid and innovative campaigns in 2023. But Tommy was everywhere all at once. He would be speaking to residents up in Pine Plains and then be down in East Fishkill knocking on doors to meet people. Then he'd meet me in Beacon at the VFW, often all on the same day. He must've put thousands of miles on his truck!

I would find Tommy sometimes at Marist, sometimes on Main Street in Poughkeepsie, and always at events and seek him out to talk affordability, the housing crisis, and expanding much-needed services around our county. He was all heart and inspiration.

And I am proud to say that Tommy is one big-ass cheerleader.

There are only a few times in your life when you get to meet somebody like Tommy. He's going to give it to you straight. He's going to be there, he's going to show up, even when it's hard – actually, *especially* when it's hard. If only we had a million more like him. I'm beyond grateful for his leadership in our community and the work he does for others -- and most of all, for the friendship of a lifetime. Tommy's that rare person you meet, the one that always makes you want to be the best version of yourself no matter what. That's because he sees you as the best version of yourself. If only we could all be a little bit more like that – our world would be a much kinder and more beautiful place.

I was devastated when Tommy lost. He was a light and a hope for many of us. And his work has inspired me to fight harder than ever before. He's a big part of why I'm running for New York State Senate for our area, District 39. This is our home. We stand united for affordability, the protection of reproductive rights, the growth of our local economy, the advancement of education, the prevention of gun violence, and the preservation of our environment. This is key to our fight. This is what we are able to do to strengthen our communities. Because we are united in our resolve, I will make sure our voices are heard up in Albany. We are advocates for our communities and we will not be going quietly.

NORA

"Do you have time for a quick call later?" Whenever I got this question from Tommy Zurhellen, I knew it would be no normal phone call. My mind began to race with ideas. Is it possible he is walking back across the country? Maybe he is biking this time? Swimming it? Tricycling, perhaps?

We hopped on the phone and he explained he had a new, special project he was working on. "I'm running for Dutchess County Executive." He always knew how to surprise me. "And I want your help."

When I began working with Tommy in 2019 on VetZero, it was clear he was someone who cared deeply about helping others. He was truly a man who walked the walk (no pun intended.) When he approached me in 2023 about working as the digital director for his campaign, I pondered if I was up to the task. I had been running my own digital marketing business for two years, but I had not worked with anyone in the political field yet. But I knew this was something Tommy believed in, so I wanted in.

We immediately got to work on our mission. We wanted to showcase that Tommy was a resident of Poughkeepsie who deeply cared about his community, not just another politician in a suit. Every Monday we sent out a campaign email written by Tommy himself. I traveled to Dutchess once a month and made videos of different events Tommy hosted and attended. Attending these events and experiencing the energy of a movement was truly uplifting.

On Election Day, I awoke at 4am in my brother's guest bedroom, even before the sun had risen, driven by the knowledge that Tommy was already out and about. I hopped in the car for an hour's drive to Rhinebeck. The roads were quiet and slick. It was still dark and the fog was so strong I could barely see some of the stoplights until I was close enough. I grabbed a coffee and thought to myself, is Tommy really going to be there at 5am with a sign? Sure enough, Tommy appeared through the morning mist, positioned at the main intersection. He proudly displayed a handmade sign, enthusiastically waving at passing cars while urging, "Make sure to get out and vote today!"

Now, while Election Day did not entirely end as we hoped, I will never forget that morning. I did not notice any other politicians with marker-stained hands traveling Dutchess County with their homemade signs. It epitomized Tommy's grassroots campaign approach. Meeting residents who passionately cared about their community inspired me. Witnessing their dedication motivated me to engage in local government. The campaign taught me that ordinary people contribute significantly to our community, even just by exercising their right to vote. Being part of this campaign was an honor, an experience etched in my memory. Tommy's campaign served as an inspiration for people in Dutchess County, and I'm confident he will continue to make positive contributions to his community.

Tommy truly walks the walk, and it makes sense. After all, he had 2,866 miles of practice.

BIG PAPA

I first heard Tommy's name from a NYS Senate candidate, my friend Karen, years back. I must have looked blank because she immediately began discussing his many good works for veterans, including the VetZero program and others. She also mentioned that he taught at Marist College, and had been helpful to not just her, but to Senator Sue Serino, Karen's then-opponent, on the broad topic of veterans' needs.

Back then, I was the Dutchess County Democrats' vice-chair, and therefore should theoretically object to him helping a Republican. But once elections are decided, you have to work with many individuals with opposite party affiliations if you want to accomplish anything. And I took this as a good sign that Tommy would cross the aisle to make sure veterans' issues were heard by those in power and solutions suggested. Though Karen lost her race, she stayed friendly with Tommy and listened and learned throughout. And she would often keep me apprised.

Our Dutchess County Executive for the last 11 years, Marc Molinaro, has had ambitions for higher office since he was elected Mayor of Tivoli, a hamlet. So, when he decided to run for Congress, it was no surprise. Molinaro had lost a special election to Pat Ryan but then ran in the general election in a different district. This set up an open seat for Dutchess County Executive for the first time in over a decade.

I've lived here for 30 years now – we still have an apartment in New York City, but I prefer the Hudson Valley. When we first bought our home, I hadn't done any research on the politics of the area. Like many from the deep South – Louisiana and Texas – I arrived assuming New York was progressive in its thinking all the way to the Canadian border. Once I started to stay for longer periods than just weekends, I began attending Town and Planning Board meetings in Hyde Park, where my husband and I reside. I also assumed that as the hometown of FDR, Hyde Park was a bastion of Democratic values. WRONG. Roosevelt never carried his hometown in any race. So we registered to vote in Dutchess, realizing our votes were needed far more up here than in Manhattan. And I became involved with local campaigns for the first time.

Sue Serino's popularity in Dutchess can seem near-fanatical at times – especially during campaign season, when pink "Go Sue!" and "Women for Serino" signs spread like mushrooms overnight. Finding a candidate to take her on would be daunting, I knew. And though I hadn't planned on ever becoming County Chair, our fabulous former Chair Julie Shiroishi had only been leading us for six months when she decided to run for an open NYS Senate seat, and I reluctantly took her place.

That's the backdrop to Tommy's race. I finally met Tommy in person at a breakfast to discuss him running. I have always been slight of build and still love clothes (a holdover after years of uniforms at Catholic schools) and I felt like Tommy was looking at me as though we were oil and water. I mean Tommy Zurhellen is a big guy with a casual style and I was a midget peacock in comparison. Tommy is also low-key when one-on-one and I'm more of a hyper type, so that first meeting was awkward in many ways. In fact, I feared he would be way too low energy to captivate voters in a way he would need to.

But then, I saw him in action, talking with a bigger group of potential supporters. From low-key to life of the party is not an exaggeration. Later, at his campaign kickoff, I felt the excitement in the air as he told jokes – he challenged the many children who came with their parents to offer a worse joke than his – and I saw the crowd exploding with laughter. Tommy was also a generous host that day. He had his fellow countywide candidates speak and that day set the tone for the remainder of the campaign: make certain that all events are child-friendly, keep the countywide team close and vocal, and maintain a civil tone.

As the political season progressed, I learned Tommy is actually exceptional in engaging even the youngest children to speak publicly. A rare talent. But he began to face internal critics for not going negative, or dishing the dirt on his opponent. Which I know was dispiriting, though there are always Democratic committee members who think they know better than the candidate. Regardless, Tommy never attacked Sue's character, and instead focused on what he would do to help residents if he were elected. He did criticize the Republicans' playbook efforts to demonize "others" and play on fear just to win – but hey, fair game. It's mostly what Republicans do these days.

Though Tommy did not win, his efforts and the door-knocking and speaking and mailers, social media, signs … I can go on, but what he did, joined by his three other countywide candidates did help our District Attorney win convincingly. Anthony Parisi became our first Democrat in that office in over a century.

Around June 2023, Tommy gave me a copy of his memoir *The Low Road*. As I read it, I came to know the intrinsic Tommy

– what makes him tick and why he is so determined to elevate fairness for all. I even slowed my reading down to maintain a feeling of connection. I told Tommy after I was done that I felt as though I had been inside his head for a week. And what that taught me, was what I had already seen during the campaign, up to Election Day. Tommy ran for all the right reasons: to raise up those less fortunate, protect seniors, ensure that children are fed and have access to a solid education, and protect the vulnerable. He will continue to do just that. It's why we are all proud to call him a friend.

ROB

Dutchess County has been a Republican stronghold for as long as I can remember. Growing up in the shadow of IBM in Hopewell Junction, I saw the corporate greed culture run amok. I saw IBM fall and the community crumble under the crunch of mass layoffs. The only good jobs that survived were Union jobs: teachers, nurses, telephone workers. Unions saved the county. My family survived thanks to the Teachers Union. I knew my future was in a Union. Fast forward a few decades and I live in a County that was saved by Union Members, yet whose Leaders ignore their voices. I am one of those voices that has spoken to deaf ears for almost 2 decades as a Business Agent and Political Coordinator for the Communications Workers of America and a Vice President for The Hudson Valley Area Labor Federation. In 2023, Labor needed a voice … and we found one.

I met Tommy Z at Michelle Hinchey's swearing-in ceremony in Saugerties. Whispers through the room were about a Challenger to Sue Serino for Dutchess County Executive being there. I scoured the room looking for the candidate I would be spending the late summer and fall knocking on doors for. The amazing Julie Shiroishi tapped me on the shoulder to introduce me to someone I (me being a giant myself) had to look up at. I shake his hand and tell him I'm Rob Pinto ... Business Agent at CWA and VP of the Area Labor Federation, and Union Proud.

"Love Unions, man!!! I'm Tommy, pleasure to meet you," he says. My job requires me to be able to smell bullshit a mile away. And usually at any event involving politics that BS meter is pinning off the charts. But I knew two things from that chat with Tommy: #1 This guy was as real as they come, and #2 This was gonna be a fun ride in Dutchess.

And man, it was.

I've been involved in politics for so long that it makes you numb. It becomes like a sporting contest. The wins are good and the losses are quickly forgotten. Win or loss, you simply move onto the next contest. But some candidates and campaigns breathe life back into you. Tommy did that. He made me believe that there is hope for the future in the County that I love.

2023 was the Year of the Strike. Tommy was everywhere supporting Workers. During the election cycle, Tommy was on the front lines with those workers, standing with CWA at Marist, SEIU at The Pines of Poughkeepsie, PPSTA at Poughkeepsie School District and with NYSNA at Vassar Hospital, just to name a few. He talked the talk and walked the walk. Tommy was a voice for Worker Justice while others were looking for Corporate Campaign checks.

Tommy ran a No-Bullshit Campaign. He tore the artificial walls down that every candidate builds. Tommy is one of us. He didn't have to pretend. Tommy is the guy pumping gas next to you at Stewart's Shops. The guy in front of you on line at Shop Rite. Tommy is the guy who raised his hand and said, "The working class needs to be heard. And I will be their voice."

JIM

It is a unique kind of pain to lose a race that you had spent the better part of nine months working to win. What was that tagline from

ABC's Wide World of Sports? "The Thrill of Victory and the Agony of Defeat." Agony might just be the right word to describe the stillness of time after the music stops on an all-consuming endeavor. It's quiet for the first time in a long while. The phone isn't blowing up. The calendar isn't full. There are no calls to make, doors to knock, emails to send, speeches to give or hands to shake. It's just you and your thoughts and it hurts more than you think it will.

Had everything gone according to plan, instead of committing these reflections to paper, I would be immersed in the task of making good on my campaign promise to transform Family Court and better the lives of vulnerable children and families. I ran my race for Dutchess County Family Court Judge for all the right reasons. I saw a glaring need for change in the failing Family Court system and I believed I could do a much better job than the incumbent to bring about that change. I've had a long career as a legal services lawyer in the courtroom representing needy New Yorkers and as an executive in government agencies enforcing laws enacted to protect the most vulnerable. As a labor leader representing lawyers for children, I fought for and won a piece of legislation that greatly increased the resources for children in Family Court.

But who knew anything about running a campaign?

I was a last-minute addition to a slate of candidates for a countywide election where more than 70,000 people would cast their vote. At the top of our ticket was Tommy running for County Executive. The pressure on him was huge. He was expected not only to win his own race in our mostly Republican county, but to carry the rest of us over the finish line. This was a mighty task and I just assumed Tommy had all the political experience in the world. I didn't know until halfway through our nine-month campaign season that Tommy's guide star was not the "win at all costs" orientation that is the hallmark of our electoral politics, but to win through the sheer strength of his will, his compassion and his humanity. That was his platform: we could be decent people.

We could care for each other; our relationship to one another was not defined by ideology or partisanship but by our shared humanity and love for our neighbor. And in this he never wavered. It was a bold and brave approach to leading a ticket and one that I sometimes found myself wishing he would abandon to instead take up the mantle of politics as blood sport.

In these moments – the moments I found myself wishing Tommy would "throw more punches" or "go for the jugular" – these are the times I had to do the most soul searching. He appealed to everything I cared about in leadership. I shared his naïve and utopian vision for what politics could be. Tommy walked across the country to try to stem the tidal wave of veteran suicide; he was the first to reach into his own pocket to help a stranger in need; he pledged his entire County Executive salary to combat food insecurity and child hunger. It eventually dawned on me that Tommy believed you couldn't govern from the heart unless you campaigned from the heart.

Some part of me however thought, "Shouldn't we be a little more pragmatic? Couldn't we sacrifice a little purity in the campaign in service of winning?" What good was it to "go high when they go low" if it meant not going anywhere at all? But take a look around. Regardless of party or ideology, no one is satisfied with their elected leaders. Too many voters believe their elected officials are corrupt or corruptible. Did all of our representatives start out this way, or was there something inherent in the quest for power that soured the soul? There's a chicken-and-egg story in here somewhere and different experiences will produce different perspectives.

I believe most people are good. Including those who run for public office. I also believe it is this innate goodness which drives people to seek office in the first place. They want to serve. I was lucky enough to share a ticket with some of the finest, most honest and committed people I have ever known. There was plenty of dirt and dirty tricks thrown in our direction, and plenty of personal attacks. But not one of us ever considered returning the favor. Thinking about it now, it surprises me how completely we stuck to the issues, how thoroughly we appealed to the good in our community, how energized we were to share our vision for the future without any reliance on tearing down the past or scuffing up the individuals who had led the county for so many years.

In my race I spent nine months talking to whomever would listen about the plight of at-risk children forced to navigate the treachery of foster care, state institutions, county officers and the labyrinth of Family Court itself; about broken families forced into a Kafkaesque limbo of maddening delays and adjournments as their children were shuffled between one inadequate solution to the next; about unmistakable racial disparities in the treatment of youth accused of crime; about victims of domestic violence, hospital records in hand, driven into shared custody arrangements with their abusers because the court couldn't make the time to hear evidence as plain as the broken noses on their faces. All of this shocked every person who heard it, regardless of party or ideology. The possibility that I could make any of this even a little bit better drove me on the campaign trail every day and drove plenty of voters to the polls. I fell less than one percent shy of victory against an entrenched incumbent. It wasn't my political party or slogans or any of that which garnered attention and votes. It was people – of all political persuasions – whose care for their community created an opening to listen.

Perhaps not the thrill of victory. But that's a win.

KENYA

My name is Kenya Gadsden. I'm married to Bernard Gadsden, my childhood sweetheart and from our union we have three beautiful children. In addition, we have been blessed with two wonderful grandchildren. My life's work has been one of service. I have cared for people with intellectual disabilities, helping them to achieve their potential for more than three decades. I created "Youth Equipped for Success" to teach critical life skills to young people, and I have served on both the Beacon School Board and Fishkill Town Board. I earned an Associate's degree from Iona College and a B.A. in Behavioral Studies from Concordia College. I am now on a quest to serve on a larger capacity in hopes of being the President of the United States of America one day.

I was proud to be one of the four people running for a Dutchess County countywide seat. During the 2023 campaign season I traveled across the county with my running mates who became my second family. We supported each other along the way, and I was cared for as if I knew the three of them all my life. We walked side by side, learning each other's platforms in a heartbeat. We could recite main points specific to each other's platforms. The season was filled with questions and concerns from each of us and we shared, encouraged, and helped each other as needed.

I recall the debate Jim Rogers had against his opponent. Jim was unstoppable, on point and in my opinion, hit the ball out of the park. Before he went on stage, he told me he had something to share with me, but would share later. I was very excited for him because at this point in the election, he was holding his own. He shared something very personal and I thought to myself, Jim was a true overcomer. I knew at this point that I was on a journey with people who really put public service ahead of themselves. The 2023 election was all that I imagined it would be. I set goals for myself and my campaign and they were achieved; even though I did not win the race, I was still a winner in so many ways. When I learned I had to have a total right hip replacement, I put people who supported me in place to be present so the voters knew I was still around. My husband Bernard and eldest daughter Pamela became my voice, and they were present at events, greeting people and sharing my vision.

I have many memorable moments while on the campaign trail, but I will sum it up with the kindness of Jim, Sinead, Anthony and Tommy, helping me to stand when I could not stand on my own for long. Many times I wanted to cry because they were strangers who immediately showed up and supported me just like my family and friends.

Each race was unique and Tommy knew what he was up against. He faced challenging people inside and outside of the Democratic party but continued to move forward in his quest to win. I was moved my Tommy's motivation and his last push to get voters out. I watched as he held up signs asking people to vote on election day, and I was excited to see where he was going to show up next to encourage people to exercise their right to vote. I believe it was very honorable of him to take the risk for the people in hopes of providing an accessible Dutchess County.

SINEAD

I'm a daughter, sister, wife, mother, attorney and most recently, the campaign manager for my husband, Anthony Parisi. This was not a role I expected, nor a role I wanted, quite frankly. But it was thrust upon me and ultimately, I surrendered my protest and embraced it.

One day in late 2022, my husband said to me, "I think I want to run for Dutchess County District Attorney. What do you think?" My brain was overloaded. I was surprised by his question since he had not mentioned it before. But my shock was quickly replaced by excitement, then fear. Excitement because I knew Anthony would be an amazing District Attorney, and fear because we both were working at the D.A.'s office and, more importantly, were parents to two small children, Seraphina (age 4) and Giuliana (age 2.) I had zero idea what this potential endeavor would entail or what toll it could take on our young family. But without much hesitation, I told Anthony we, as a family, would be there to support him. Little did I know I had gotten myself (and us) into!

I recall meeting Anthony's countywide running mates – Tommy for County Executive, James Rogers for Family Court Judge, and Kenya Gadsden for County Clerk. I knew right away these were some special people who truly wanted to make a difference and serve their community. It was at Tommy's campaign kickoff event that my husband first introduced me as his campaign manager. At that time, it was a joke – or so I thought! Things took off from there and I realized my title of campaign manager was not a joke but reality. From that point in April until November, things never stopped. But I can also say, I became part of the team: keeping the schedule, taking pictures, and cheering them on. Whatever the team needed, I tried my best to be there for them. This was not an easy task with two small children, but we made it work.

The pace, schedule and stress were something that only someone who has run for office can truly comprehend. But I can say confidently these four county candidates handled themselves with dignity and grace and somehow managed to temper the stress with humor, especially Tommy. As the saying goes, "If you don't laugh, you'll cry." I think that saying came from someone running for public office!

I firmly believe that children have a sixth sense when it comes to adults. I think their innocence allows them to see deep inside a grown-up and they gravitate to that goodness they see. Maybe it's being able to see the child inside and relate, but whatever it is, my girls saw the heart and kindness in Tommy from the start. Almost every event Tommy held had a joke competition which usually entailed Tommy and any kids present telling their "best" joke. I think this was when Tommy first started to steal the hearts of my two daughters. At Tommy's kickoff event, Seraphina went up to Tommy to tell her best joke. "What do you call an alligator that investigates crime?"

Wait for it ... an investi-gator!

Tommy had prizes for all the kids who told a joke. It made their day! No matter the event or how many people were there, Tommy always had time for my kids. And they genuinely would be excited to see "Mr. Tommy" and share some ice cream!

Tommy Zurhellen might be the most humble, down-to-earth, kind soul I have ever met. He was running for a major county office, but he never lost sight of what was important and WHO was important. He stayed true to himself while campaigning and also continued all his charitable endeavors, but also had time for ice cream with my kids. Tommy might not have won the election for Dutchess County Executive, but he won the hearts of my family. We are all better people for having spent most of 2023 together and I am honored to now call Tommy my friend.

CHRIS

My name is Chris Drago and I live in the Town of Stanford, NY. I grew up in Dutchess County and ran for the Dutchess County Legislature in 2023 in District 19 which encompasses Milan, Pine Plains, Millerton, North East, Stanford and Eastern Red Hook. I won the primary election with 78% of the vote and went on to unseat the longtime Chairman of the Dutchess County Legislature during the general election in November.

This was my first time running for office and I'm thankful for all of the support I got along the way. It was comforting to meet Tommy and the other candidates for Countywide candidates early in the campaign and it was nice to see them often out on the campaign trail together. "Not for oneself but for all" is a phrase that means a lot to me and helps guide the work I do. Tommy lives this motto everyday and it was inspiring to learn about his journey and what motivated him to run for elected office. Tommy was always quick to offer help, and showed up frequently to meet people across Northern Dutchess County to learn what makes our part of the county unique. Tommy certainly took the high road during his campaign, which is something important for us all to keep in mind no matter what we may pursue in our lives.

MICHELLE

Even though Tom had been a member of the Health and Fitness Center I work at for years, I never really knew him. When he walked across America and I saw his picture everywhere, I recognized him from the gym and thought, like many others did, how is he going to walk across the country? He's a big guy who appears to move very slow. I was amazed when I heard he did.

I didn't really see Tom at the gym after his walk across America and then COVID hit and gyms were shut down for almost 6 months. As members came back to the gym, there were less of them which made it easier to get to know the ones who did come back. A few years after everything reopened, I saw Tom come into the gym one morning and tell the Front Desk staff he was going to take the class. The class was my class! I was thinking, is he really serious? The class is a fast-moving cardio class using a step. Tom, to me, did not seem fast moving. While I'm always encouraged when members want to try something new and want to move, I thought well, he will probably try this once and decide to never do it again. I was totally wrong and I'm so glad I was! Not only did Tom keep coming back to the class, he started taking other classes at the encouragement of other members he met in class. When Tom first took my class, he would be in the back of the room and keep to himself. He would do the class, but his movement was fairly slow. Two years later, I'm amazed not only at how much better Tom is moving, but at the community of friends he has in class. They even got him to start taking one of the dance classes!

I will admit, at first, I was a little nervous when Tom was taking my class because I felt like this guy does so much good for the community, I almost felt intimidated talking to him (his stature adds to his intimidation). Once you get to know him though, he puts you at ease and has become a great friend to talk to. I truly admire all the work he does for the community, especially for our Veterans. I'm so glad Tom decided to come into the gym one day and say I'm going to take the class. Not only do I have another participant in my class who is trying to stay active, but I've met a wonderful person who I consider a friend. Keep moving Tom! Your friends and I will see you next week in class!

CHRISTA

I have had the privilege of Tommy Zurhellen being my dear friend for over five years and when I look back on what he's accomplished in that relatively short time, I am simply amazed. Amazed but not surprised, to say the least. It was back in 2018 when he reached out to me as the new Commander of the VFW, to see how Hudson River Housing and the VFW could work together to help veterans and our community at large. From that very first day, I was so taken back by Tommy's commitment to *action*. Many people talk about doing things to make a difference, but Tommy actually does things! It's funny to think back on that first day. Although his enthusiasm and passion were so evident, even I could not comprehend that I would be writing this page for his *second* book since I've known him!

First walking nearly 3,000 miles across America to raise awareness for homeless veterans in our country through the VetZero Project he created. Then writing an incredible book, *The Low Road*, about the experience which raised funds to launch a highly successful free ride program for veterans. Next, running for public office as Dutchess County Executive! And now he's writing a book about that remarkable experience. All the while remaining wonderfully humble and kind and guiding students as a well-respected English professor at an esteemed institution like Marist. Talk about making a difference!

We are truly blessed to have a person like Tommy, with such passion and determination to make a positive difference in the world. I am beyond proud and honored to call him my friend. Congratulations Tommy on another successful adventure. I cannot wait for what is NEXT!

BORIS

It turns out that compassion, honor and integrity are three terrible traits to have if you're trying to win an election. A shrewd political candidate for County Executive would have drooled at the chance of being given a live microphone on the number-one radio station in the county they were running in. How did Tom Zurhellen spend this precious airtime? By inviting the commander of a local VFW chapter to plea for help finding a new location for his post, telling our listeners about the new one-stop center for veteran services and reminding local vets they can bring their families to a Marist basketball game for free.

The weekly Veteran Report has become an extremely popular segment on The Boris and Robyn Show. When Tom confided in me that he was going to run for County Executive I immediately drew up a draft email to his opponent, offering her equal airtime in the event Tom would venture off-topic from his weekly discussion with veterans' advocates about local events and resources.

That email was never sent.

But that's Tom; someone who wouldn't even entertain the idea of using his platform for political gain. A man who would be out late into the evening speaking at a political rally and still wake up at the crack of dawn to come on our show to talk about anything else than his campaign. A candidate who ran for office with compassion, honor and integrity. Could someone like that ever get elected to political office? Sadly, I think we all know the answer.

ROBYN

When Commander Tom invited me to write a little something for this book, I thought to myself... how can I put into words what a great guy this is? But I'll give it a shot. Here in the Hudson Valley, Commander Tom has single-handedly raised awareness of Veterans and their lives while and after serving our country. I've always appreciated our Veterans, but had no idea about the depression and homelessness that so many suffer after they've served until I met Tom. If I wasn't aware, how many of our listeners weren't either? Tom would give you the shirt off his back whether you're a Veteran or not. And that's the kind of man that our Veterans deserve going to bat for them.

Tom is a great asset to our Veterans and to our community, and I'm proud to call him my colleague and my friend.

RENEE

The 2023 election for Dutchess County Executive was like nothing I had ever seen in my decades of work in human services. While access to government leaders has been steadily improving in recent years, this particular election surfaced a certain humanity that took me by surprise, and it changed the rules of engagement. Months prior to the heavy campaigning, I sought advice from a friend in Albany who had been working in politics for decades. I wanted to understand how we could leverage this campaign to bring attention to the issue of food insecurity that would change

After/Words

the landscape in a profound way. I never got the chance. In fact, I never even needed the chance because Tommy was way ahead of me!

Both candidates had a deep awareness of the issue of food insecurity. They had organized food drives, volunteered in our programs, and cared about the issue on a personal level. It would have been so easy for them to leave it at that and keep the issue where it had always been: a charitable endeavor. Yet, we decided to meet with each candidate separately and provide them with the exact same information. This was a perfect opportunity to challenge each of them to make commitments to solve the entirely solvable problem of hunger in our community. Each meeting went well, and both agreed that, if elected, they would do more to ensure people had the food they need.

Months later I was attending an event and was asked by an elected official I had known for years, "Why is Tommy saying there are hungry children in Dutchess County?" That was the first time anyone in local government had asked me about the issue of food insecurity in my three years of leading a food security organization. Until that moment the issue of hunger in our community, and feeding people in need, was seen as a charitable enterprise and organizations providing food support to the youngest, oldest and everyone in between were expected to rely upon our 'philanthropic base'. While there are so many problems with viewing the provision of food as charity and not a human right, the challenge facing us post-COVID was that the numbers of people who don't have enough food, children among them, was outpacing our ability to fundraise and purchase the food people need. There had been exceptions, of course. Then Mayor of the City of Poughkeepsie Rob Rolison directed significant support for infrastructure for food providers, and the county stepped up with financing meals during the worst of the pandemic. But, until this specific election, and until Tommy, the issue of hunger and food insecurity remained a problem to be solved by the volunteers and donors of our community.

In so many ways, Tommy won for the community without winning the election. It's because of his humanity, along with the genuine friendship and respect he shared with his opponent, that hearts were disarmed, and minds were opened. Our government leaders felt compelled to understand the social issues that create and sustain poverty and opened the doors to real conversation and strategizing solutions. For the first time in our organization's 50-year history, there is a seat at the table where change happens, and problems find answers. In my opinion, this is the real win.

CHLOE

I had the honor to follow Tommy's incredible campaign journey, it's clear how profoundly he has impacted our community. Tommy's campaign was never just about winning an election; it was a heartfelt mission to uplift everyone in the community. Tommy's dedication was evident throughout his campaign. He faced local issues, always striving to bring real, meaningful change in our daily lives. His passion and commitment were clearly shown in every initiative and interaction, reflecting his deep understanding of the challenges faced by our community. Tommy's genuine care and selflessness have created a lasting impact. His campaign stands as a powerful example of true leadership and making a positive difference. Thank you, Tommy for being a dear friend and for being a beacon of hope and change for us all.

MALIA

I heard about Tommy Zurhellen before I met him. "The guy who walked across America for veterans" is well-known in the Hudson Valley, especially to veterans like me. I was pleased when I learned he had agreed to join our Congressman's Veterans and Military Families Advisory Board, where I would have the chance to meet him and work with him.

At the first VAMFAB meeting, we all went around the room introducing ourselves, starting with our Congressman (a West Point grad and Army vet,) then me (another Army vet,) and around the room to several other Army vets and a few Air Force and Marine vets too. Finally, we got around to Tommy, who had been waiting quietly. "US NAVY!!!" he announced with a defiant grin, as if daring us to challenge him while simultaneously signaling he would enjoy making short work of that challenge. We all cracked up, and then got down to the important work before us.

That first meeting was the perfect introduction to Tommy. He was the largest person in the room and a true local celebrity, yet what stood out most about him was his humility and the care he took in listening to others. I soon realized there is no artifice with this man; he is as genuine as they come, and his authenticity springs directly from his quiet and unerring dedication to service.

"Service" is a word that perhaps gets overused. Or it is so ubiquitous that we don't stop to contemplate what it really means. Tommy is a creative writing professor in addition to a veterans' activist. Despite the rarity of that combination, those two attributes are mutually reinforcing insofar as they require you to give something of yourself to the work and to prioritize all the stories, told and untold, past and future, of the people we encounter. I don't think it is possible to either be a successful activist or a successful writer – to serve – without a basic level of optimism. Otherwise, what could we hope to accomplish, and why would we be investing so much effort?

Probably few civilians would describe members of the military as optimists. But I think at our heart that's what we are, because we are animated by the belief that together we can accomplish just about anything. Together we can solve any problem. Together we are damn near invincible and can guarantee that the things worth dying and fighting for will long endure. People don't usually join the military and run into battle because they think the world is going to end – quite the opposite. That is why I find it uniquely inspiring when veterans run for office, a circumstance that is increasingly rare because there are fewer veterans among us as time goes on.

It is fitting that Tommy is calling this book about his political campaign The High Road, because that is what I saw him take throughout his campaign, not as a manner of strategy or tactics, but as a manifestation of the contribution he is already making in the world through his writing and his activism. I actually looked forward to getting his campaign newsletters – which I have never said about any other political literature I have ever received – because they were so heartfelt, empathetic, and thoughtful, and they respected the intelligence of his readers.

Tommy has shown us the High Road in many different ways and places. We are all lucky to have the chance to walk with him on any part of it.

MEGAN

My name is Megan Deichler and I am currently a council member in the City of Poughkeepsie. I met Tommy on the campaign trail leading up to the November 2023 election while I was running for a second term on the City Common Council. The first time I heard Tommy speak was during a Poughkeepsie Democratic Committee meeting. I had never heard of him before, despite his impressive resume and the incredible feat he accomplished walking across the country and raising awareness for veterans. During this first meeting, he impressed me with his vision, but I was extremely skeptical given his limited experience in politics. Once the campaign got started and I got to know Tommy better, I realized there was something special there – he was not a typical politician like most I had known, he was running an altruistic campaign, truly wanting to help the people, without ego or aggrandizement motivating his run.

The nature of politics often attracts individuals who win elections due to popularity but may be completely unqualified to make important decisions that impact their constituents' lives. Politics also too often attracts narcissistic characters who wouldn't make it far in the "real world" but got lucky enough to convince the majority of voters to elect them to decision-making bodies. Tommy embodied none of that. He was running a campaign of kindness with a mission to help the most disadvantaged people in our community. Not only did he have a heart, but he also had no shortage of intelligent ideas that could really improve quality of life for a lot of people in Dutchess County. We worked together attending meet-and-greet events, along with other obligatory campaign activities, and every time Tommy spoke, I gained a greater level of respect for him and saw him as a unique politician who really just wanted to help people.

There were certain groups in our community that had supported Republican candidates without question for decades– never even giving Democrats a chance to make their case. One anecdote that stands out to me is hearing about Tommy requesting a meeting with one such group. This group had already made a commitment to endorse his opponent despite never giving Tommy a chance, and he still wanted to meet with them. During their meeting, he spoke about the "D" after his name standing for decency and explained in empathetic terms why he took certain stances on issues whether it be food insecurity or support for asylum seekers arriving in Poughkeepsie. This group of folks were left nearly speechless and had a hard time keeping smiles off their faces as Tommy made his pitch.

This is an example of the effect he had on people he met

throughout the campaign. Overall, campaigning is not easy and in the case of a county with almost 300,000 residents, even if you knock on doors every single day for a year before the election, mathematically, you still only reach a fraction of the electorate. I believe if more people had the pleasure of getting to know Tommy and hearing about his work and his vision firsthand, we would have had a different outcome.

LISA

As a longtime disability rights advocate, I have met countless political officials, community leaders and local and state human rights activists over the last two decades. But this past year, I had the distinctive pleasure of meeting Tommy Zurhellen.

I am Executive Director of a Poughkeepsie-based disability rights organization, Taconic Resources for Independence, Inc. (TRI) and our work is to promote the full inclusion of individuals with disabilities in all aspects of community life. One way to do this is to raise public awareness, which is how I met Tommy. For the last two years in June, TRI has partnered with the Home of FDR National Historic Site to host our Inclusion Festival event to promote community-based living options for Dutchess residents with disabilities and to show case supportive community leaders. Tommy was in the midst of his campaign for Dutchess County Executive and thought his attendance at our event would be a great opportunity for him to meet and greet attendees and answer any questions they may have.

My colleague John assisted Tommy with his campaign and arranged an introductory meeting with him at my office prior to our June event at the FDR site. I was thrilled for the chance to meet him and was eager to hear about his views fir implementing public policies to promote and enhance compliance with the

Americans with Disabilities Act. Tommy arrived at my office that day, casually dressed wearing his VFW hat, and graciously introduced himself while expressing his admiration for our organization's mission as a community advocate for individuals with disabilities. During our meeting, I briefed Tommy on some of the many challenges individuals with disabilities encounter on a daily basis, including lack of affordable and accessible housing and access barriers to stores, restaurants and recreational venues, which exclude them from participating fully in community life. His response: "I will immediately appoint a Chief Disability Officer for Dutchess County." He explained the mission of this office would be to make all public spaces in the county accessible to all people and "second, ensure the voices of our neighbors with disabilities are heard."

As a result of that meeting, John and I decided to create a voter guide with Tommy's views on disability policies. Of course, Tommy agreed and we were able to distribute it over our social media network and at community events. When he attended our Inclusion Festival later that June, he was intent on learning as much as he could – firsthand – about the concerns affecting individuals with disabilities and referenced them in his July 4th campaign newsletter, "A Real Day of Independence." That message was a clarion call to remove the myriad barriers to full community inclusion persons with disabilities face. It articulated what the role of municipal leaders should be in serving the needs of the constituents: listening with intent.

Thank you, Tommy for your gracious message in acknowledging the struggles of the disability community and for eloquently defining the deeper meaning of independence and what it represents for our community. To me, you exemplify what it is to be a genuine, dedicated public servant who truly walks the talk. Thank you for listening.

HEIDI & MIKE

The consolation prize for putting your heart and soul into a campaign that should have won, but didn't, is the truly wonderful people you meet along the way. We proudly worked harder, knocked on more doors, made more calls, and hosted and attended more events in 2023 than ever before. Our six candidates were not just running to put a "D" on their office door. Each one had concrete and feasible plans to make their little corner of the world better for its residents. They were inspirational, relatable, funny, warm, sincere "doers" who have been doing good things for a long, long time. They each poured everything they had into bringing their messages out to the public while sticking to Tommy's mantra, "The 'D' stands for Decency."

One of the six, and the author of this book, stood out among the others as an unbelievable dynamo of public service. Most people like Tommy display a frenetic, whirling dervish sort of energy. Tommy's energy, however, hits more like a fine Bourbon. Calm and smooth on the outside that later translates to a deep fire and profound effect. Our committee chose him to be our 2023 Gertie Strum Award recipient. This prestigious award highlights the "power of one." Gertie was already well into her senior citizen years when she single-handedly catalyzed the revitalization of the Union Vale Democratic Committee. We witnessed Tommy doing the same kind of thing, not because he was running for County Executive, but in addition to running for County Executive. Tommy makes those around him want to do more! Not because he shames them or begs them, just because he's an amazing example. Gertie would have absolutely loved Tommy and you could almost feel her smiling down as we presented him with our honorary gavel of activism!

The only time I saw Tommy display a negative emotion was at a big countywide meeting. Tommy arrived a little late. He had obviously been busy all day. For the first time, he seemed tired. Someone shouted out for him to make a speech – he obliged. Then, someone wanted to know when he was going to "take the gloves off" and "go after" his opponent. Across his face flashed annoyance and irritation as he once again stated the "D" stands for Decency and a refusal to sling negativity. Now there were probably more than a few people in that room who actually wanted Tommy to point out the many shortcomings of his Republican adversary. But pointing this out simply isn't Tommy and it will never be. Engaging in this would have been artificial, petty and frankly, too political to fit in with his character.

Tommy once said to a group that was heavily Republican that if you don't want to help people in your community that need helping, then we don't want your vote. And that, in my opinion, seems to be the major difference between "D" and "R." In our little town of Union Vale, pretty much all you need is an "R" by your name on the ballot in order to win. It is an uphill battle every election to run our "D" candidates against the "R" machine. But we keep going. We keep bringing our message of "we" not "me." We have ideas to move forward, not stare wistfully at the past. So, for now, we will take inspiration from those, like Tommy, who run alongside us on the correct side of history and gear up for the next one! It is an absolute joy and honor to know Tommy as a candidate, a fellow activist, and a friend.

TED

The eight months I served as Tommy's campaign manager were the most exhilarating and busy I ever experienced. Accompanying Tommy through Dutchess County, watching him interact with people, "kissing hands and shaking babies," his face aglow with enthusiasm and optimism, made me hopeful not just for the people of Dutchess County, but all people throughout this nation.

Tommy was the type of candidate we need more of in America: honest, plain-spoken, folksy, with genuine compassion for those less fortunate, the marginalized, the too-often ignored.

Yet those qualities only go far. A sincere candidate needs a sincere message. And's Tommy's message was sincere: "This year the 'D' stands for "decency."

He got voters as upset over the unhoused being kept in the old county jail as he was.

He got them to know they had been cheated out of $25 million when the prior county executive handed federal relief money over to the New York Yankees to subsidize the Hudson Valley Renegades minor league baseball team that played at a stadium county residents couldn't even call Dutchess Stadium anymore after it had been sold to Heritage Financial bank.

He urged voters to know the "fear" County Executive O'Neill wanted to instill in them over a couple dozen asylum seekers housed in the Red Roof Inn awaiting their immigration papers was a cheap distraction that would not be tolerated in a Zurhellen administration.

He wanted Dutchess County's youth to know they wouldn't have to leave the place they grew up for work but would be educated at home for a workforce that would make them the future drivers of the county economy.

Tuition-free enrollment at Dutchess Community College. More financial support for local businesses. Transforming the solid-waste incinerator into a recycling center that would clean up the environment. More support for the unhoused and veterans. Unwavering support for local unions. And, yes, *donating his County Executive salary to organizations combatting food insecurity.*

He pledged to do all these things, and more.

It was an honor, a pleasure, and a privilege to serve as Tommy's campaign manager.

Dutchess County is better for having had a candidate like Tommy. He set an example others will no doubt follow. All people should be so fortunate to have a candidate like Tommy taking a chance on trying to make the world a better place, starting at home. One road at a time.

THE FIANCÉE

I was blessed to be in a committed relationship with Tommy for 8 whole years; and to me he is just Tom. When we knew our relationship was coming to a close, my greatest fear was losing him as a friend. Thankfully that never happened. When he chose to run for office, I knew that I wanted to support him any way I could. I showed up for political gatherings, I went door to door with palm cards, I hosted a wine and cheese gathering to meet and greet the candidate, I planted lawn signs. I was confident that the hard working, man of integrity I loved would serve Dutchess County with all of his heart soul, mind and strength. Dutchess county lost out in November but because of Tom's dedication our democratic base has definitely grown.

GREG GATTINE
RADIO WOODSTOCK 100.1 WDST

Thirty years ago, Dickey Betts wrote a great song for The Allman Brothers Band called Seven Turns. It was inspired by his Navajo friend who explained to him the 7 times in life when you make a decision on which path to take.

I don't know which Turn Tommy was on at that point, but I was on the one where I was a radio DJ in Poughkeepsie. I may have seen Tommy around over the years at a concert or a bar or a party, I don't remember. I may have met him at a VFW picnic one of my ex-wives asked me to DJ.

I do remember finding out about Tommy when he was walking across the country raising awareness for veterans. I have many friends who have DRIVEN across the country multiple times, and a couple who have hitch-hiked it. I drove it once taking the southern route in the summer in a 1990 Toyota pickup with no AC and no power anything. I barely made it. If you had asked me how long it would take to walk across the country at that point, I probably would have said three years.

Soon after Tommy made it back to Poughkeepsie, he emailed me and asked to come on Radio Woodstock to help promote the VetZero program. I love people who contribute to society and make the world a better place, so I said yes right away. I connected with the man immediately. I wanted all my listeners to hear about his mission and intentions. After a couple of appearances, he told me about the next Turn he was taking: running for Dutchess County Executive.

I was quite surprised initially but quickly realized Tommy is exactly the kind of person I would vote for. He certainly walks the walks. Could he talk the talk that wins elections? I knew he could connect with voters, but did he have enough gas left? Did he have enough time? Did he have any money?

Well, it turns out he had enough gas.

I've had many politicians on the air over the years. Democrats, Republicans, Independents (mostly Democrats.) Bernie Sanders, Howard Dean, John Kerry, to name a few. I loved Maurice Hinchey's monthly appearances. These days I have his daughter Michelle on the air often. She represents the 41st Senate district in New York. And Congressman Pat Ryan is on air with us every month.

Tommy doesn't talk like a politician. He talks like he's my friend who wants to come pick me up to go help someone else. During his campaign he would come on the show and talk about the issues: the environment, the schools, the guns, the veterans and the homeless. He didn't speak poorly about his opponent. He didn't resort to go-low politics or attack ads. He didn't win the election. This time.

I live in Ulster County these days, so I didn't get to vote for Tommy. I did get to vote for Jen Metzger who has some progressive ideas for our county that I'm more than willing to help her inform our listeners about. As Tommy has pointed out many times on the air, politics as usual won't cut it anymore. If Tommy wants to run again, I stand behind him.

It's been a privilege to get to know the man and support his efforts on these last couple Turns. "May the Lord bless you and keep you" – Numbers 6:24

PHOTOGRAPHS

"Why is your headshot in a window?" Big Papa asked. I didn't want to tell him what the rest of the photo studio looked like ...

Even Nora's cat liked our Team Tommy shirts. Two paws up!

When you cradle your very first lawn sign in your arms, it's a special moment.

My good friend (and fellow veteran) Pat Ryan stopped by my birthday party in April.

Even with all the campaign events, I still made time to fulfill my commitments to the community, like this Fill Tommy's Truck event to benefit Grace Smith House.

Talking about the walk with Senator Gillibrand at the VA was an absolute honor.

Avengers assemble! The Dutchess dream team looking hungry at Kenya's fundraiser.

Photographs

Here's proof I wore a blazer at least once! At the Salute to Labor event with Lt. Gov. Antonio Delgado.

It doesn't matter the journey: meeting veterans will always be my favorite part. At the Hyde Park Memorial Day parade.

As the months went on, I got much better at stumping. At the Clinton Democrats event.

Trying to win the elusive alpaca vote in Hyde Park.

Photographs

The senior picnics turned out to be a wonderful way to meet new folks.

The Tuccis in Union Vale were helpful from start to finish, hosting events at their home.

I gained a new appreciation for our labor unions. At a Team Tommy event in Poughkeepsie. Union Strong!

"Union Busting is Disgusting!" Walking the picket line with 1199 SEIU in Poughkeepsie.

My friend Yvette Valdés Smith does the work! Picking up trash together at the VA.

Telling the truth at the Chamber of Commerce debate in Poughkeepsie.

I felt lonely up on stage at the NAACP debate after my opponent failed to show up.

Our four countywide candidates Jim Rogers, Anthony Parisi, Kenya Gadsden and myself sharing a moment late in the campaign. We look confident!

My friend Chris Drago ran his own campaign of kindness against the incumbent in his Dutchess County Legislature district. Congrats Chris!

Senator Michelle Hinchey always gave me a boost on the trail, even though many others had turned away. "Keep doing what you're doing!"

Candidates have to blow off steam on the campaign trail somehow! Photobombing Robin Lois here. (Sorry, Robin.)

A few minutes to go before polls close on Election Night. Getting interviewed on the platform in Poughkeepsie.

Photographs

Look at my face! So tired. Waiting for the results to come in at Democrat HQ.

Anthony Parisi being sworn in as Dutchess County District Attorney with his wife Sinead and family. A proud moment for all of us.

In 2024, my friend and partner-in-kindness Yvette Valdés Smith ran an amazing campaign for state senate, fighting for social justice. She will always be my hero.

ACKNOWLEDGMENTS

THIS BOOK is dedicated to the thirteen million children in America who go hungry each day, as well as the everyday heroes trying to do something about it. In some small way, I hope *The High Road* helps to raise awareness on the vital issue of food insecurity in our country. If you live in the Hudson Valley, I encourage you to visit the Food Bank of the Hudson Valley website at www.foodbankofhudsonvalley.org to join the fight against food insecurity in our local communities. And if you live elsewhere in America, please visit the No Kid Hungry website www.nokidhungry.org or the Feeding America website www.feedingamerica.org today. Together, we can make a difference.

A book about kindness is, by definition, an exercise in collaboration and community. Writing such a book would be futile without recognizing the energy, guidance and support of countless others. There are too many people to list individually, so instead I will be brief. First, thanks to my campaign team of Ted, Nora and Emma. It was an honor to witness your hard work and creativity on our Little Campaign That Could. Thanks to my countywide colleagues Anthony, Sinead, Kenya, Bernard, Jim and Nicole for becoming my extended family in 2023 and beyond. Thanks to all the electeds and local candidates who took the time to support our efforts last year, especially my friend and favorite partner-in-kindness, Yvette Valdés Smith. Thank you to all the Dutchess Democrats who worked tirelessly behind the scenes to help our campaign, especially the Michaels and the Tuccis. Thanks to all my union heroes, especially Rob at CWA. Union Strong! Thanks to all the community partners who do the real work of kindness every day, including Lisa at TRI and Renee at Dutchess Outreach. Thank you to all the new friends I made while walking the campaign trail last year, especially Michelle and Costa. And much gratitude to my OG family and friends for your continued bedrock support, especially Mom and Dad, Christa, Jeff, Heather and first-time voter Aidan, for teaching an old man to embrace the sour. Finally, thanks to Adriann for using all your powers, and all your skills, to edit this hot mess of a book.

Grandma, I was thinking of you as I wrote this book. Hope this one makes you proud.

REQUIRED READING

WRITING ANY book requires a great deal of reading and research. As we tell our students at Marist, good writers must be good readers, too. Here's a list of some of the books I read while writing *The High Road*, in no particular order. They have all been helpful or inspiring to me in different ways. If you are thinking about running for office, I encourage you to begin by reading the stories and accounts of others, before forging your own path.

Across That Bridge by John Lewis
I Swear by Katie Porter
The Truths We Hold: An American Journey by Kamala Harris
The Joy of Politics by Amy Klobuchar
Be Useful by Arnold Schwarzenegger
A Full Life by Jimmy Carter
Oath and Honor by Liz Cheney
Grateful American by Gary Sinise
The Inferno by Dante Alighieri

ABOUT THE AUTHOR

Tommy Zurhellen is the author of the award-winning Messiah Trilogy of novels, which reimagine the life of Jesus in modern-day rural America: *Nazareth, North Dakota* (2011), *Apostle Islands* (2012), and *Armageddon, Texas* (2014), all from Atticus Books. His memoir *The Low Road: Walking the Walk for Veterans* (2021) follows his solo trek across America in the summer of 2019 to raise awareness on veteran suicide and homelessness. His short stories have appeared widely in *Carolina Quarterly, Passages North, Crab Creek Review, Quarterly West*, and elsewhere. Since 2019, Tommy has delivered a weekly veterans update as "Commander Tom" on 101.5FM WPDH with the Boris & Robyn Show, and he has also appeared regularly on 100.1FM WDST Radio Woodstock with his friend Greg Gattine. He served honorably in the United States Navy as a Nuclear Electrician onboard the USS Truxtun and USS California. With the help of the G.I. Bill, he received his M.F.A. from the University of Alabama and has taught Creative Writing at Marist College for the past twenty years. *The High Road* is his second memoir.

www.ingramcontent.com/pod-product-compliance
Lightning Source LLC
Chambersburg PA
CBHW031434160426
43195CB00010BB/732